For Dorothy Carm
Best Wishes
Dorothy Williams
2/12/04

AGENTS THAT FLY

A BREED APART I I

Charles H. Weems
Retired U.S. Treasury
ATF Agent

SSI Publications

Copyright © 1993
by Charles H. Weems

Library of Congress Card Catalog Number 93-086815

ISBN 0-9634357-2-8   (Hardcover)
ISBN 0-9634357-3-6   (Softcover)

Published in the United States by
SSI Publications
P.O. Box 130
Luttrell, Tennessee 37779

Printed in the United States of America
by Rose Printing Company Inc.
Tallahassee, Florida 32314

Photographs by various Treasury Agents
Cover design and artwork by SSI Publications

The experiences related by the author are true and the actual names of federal, state and local officers involved in these cases have been used. The names of most of the violators have been changed as a courtesy to their families.

DEDICATED TO

Robert J. Williams
Todd W. McKeehan
Steven D. Willis
Conway LeBleu

February 28, 1993

And the hundreds of other ATF agents killed in the line of duty.

1.

CHANCE ENCOUNTER

JIM, I THINK you'd better restart the engine," I suggested. We were down to 1,000 feet above the ground and descending at a rate of 500 feet per minute. Two minutes to touchdown and the propeller was dead still.

The flight had started that morning from Gunn Airfield, a small private airstrip seven miles east of Atlanta. Jim Daniels and I were checking out the prolific moonshining area north of Atlanta in Dawson and Lumpkin counties. It was the early fall of 1964 and there was a brisk feeling of winter soon to come to the mountains of north Georgia.

I had been a special agent with the U.S. Treasury Department for ten years. Every day was filled with new challenges and the time had passed quickly. Although my life had been filled with excitement and adventure from the time I was 16, when I sailed as a merchant seaman, then joined the Army and served overseas as a paratrooper, at last I was getting the opportunity to fulfil a lifelong dream—I was learning to fly.

Jim, a Boeing 727 Captain with Eastern Airlines, was busy trying to restart the engine of the Cessna 150. We continued to lose altitude. He had deliberately stopped the engine, saying that he wanted to show me how a glider flew. Looking back, I know that he was trying to build my confidence in the safety of airplanes, but at the time all I could think of was seeing that propeller turn again.

The starter groaned—RRRM—RRMM—RRMMMMM.

"Maybe if you primed it?" I asked hesitantly, knowing this was like a little leaguer telling Mickey Mantle how to hit. I began to look around for a place to land. Jim was looking, too. We would hit the ground within one minute if he didn't get that engine started.

"I don't want to flood it," Jim answered, but to my relief he reached over and hit the primer, injecting raw gasoline into the cylinders. The engine roared to life 500 feet above a small pasture.

"Whew."

Neither of us said much on the way back to Atlanta, and Jim didn't give me any more demonstrations of glider flight.

★ ★ ★

A week later I was telling Henry Gastley of my frustration and disappointment in not being able to make a conspiracy case against J.R. Turner, one of the largest moonshine kingpins in the United States. My anger was accentuated by the fact that one of our own agents had apparently been on J.R.'s payroll, negating years of intense investigative work by several ATF agents, myself included. That agent was no longer a problem, thanks to top-notch detective work by ATF Agent Jim King and John Crunkleton of the DeKalb County Vice Squad.

"Charley, they were making liquor before you were born and they'll be making it after you're dead," Henry commented.

Gastley was a man of enormous experience in fighting the never-ending battle with moonshiners in the southeast, having begun as a prohibition agent and progressed through the ranks to a supervisory position in ATF. Even though I knew he was right, I could not accept the idea that we would never stop the flow of rotgut whiskey that had ruined so many lives over the years.

I grew up during the Depression era of the 1930's in Clayton County, Georgia, a rural county south of Atlanta. It was not a pleasant time. I remember vividly the muddy still hands, smelling of liquor and mash, who stopped by our old wood frame service station. They always scared me. As a four-year-old only child in the year 1932, I felt that these men were a threat to my father and mother, who were just barely getting by, trying to make payments on three acres of land and keep food on the table. On occasion they would give my father a one-gallon can of moonshine, which he immediately placed in a charred keg to be hidden in a hen's nest in the chicken house.

Sooner or later Pop would drink enough to get mean and then he and Mom would have a violent "cuss fight." Others who have experienced this in their childhood may understand the sadness, heartbreak and fear felt by a four-year-old in this situation. I grew up dreading Christmas because people were always drinking. It was a miserable season for me and I still get very depressed at Christmastime after all these years.

In the 1950's and '60's moonshining was prolific in every southeastern state, with Georgia and North Carolina leading the pack. There has always been an argument about which state produced the most moonshine, but never any question as to where the most moonshine was consumed—Atlanta won, hands down.

The Atlanta area was a hunter's paradise for ATF agents. There was every size illegal distillery imaginable and violators operated in all facets of the business. Some large organizations produced in excess of 1,000 gallons of whiskey per *day* or 30,000 gallons per month, and trying to stop the flow of more than a million gallons of moonshine a year into Atlanta alone was a tremendous and exciting task. The job was like a continuous chase, chess game and physical contact sport all at once. We were given free rein as long as we produced cases and submitted the never-ending paperwork on time.

Moonshiners exhibited all levels of intelligence, ability and cunning. Agents did, too. I fell somewhere in the middle with reference to intelligence, although I felt I was one of the best when it came to field work.

In the cunning area I was not so hot, but I did manage to surprise myself at times.

My first meeting with Jim Daniels had been through John Guy, Area Supervisor for the Bureau of Alcohol, Tobacco and Firearms (ATF). I was a Regional Special Agent for ATF, working out of the Atlanta office. John and I became close friends while investigating several extremely sensitive cases: the death of Area Supervisor Doug Denney; an obstruction of justice case against a paid government informant; and the shooting of three moonshiners and the subsequent death of ATF Special Agent Gene Howell. Jim and John were neighbors who had met across the back fence. John soon discovered that Jim was looking for adventure.

One day Jim commented, "John, I was flying a Piper Cub over Newton County yesterday when I saw two men come out of the woods and load something on a pickup truck. I dropped down closer. When they saw me they jumped in the truck and took off. I chased them for the fun of it but stopped when it seemed they might crash into some innocent vehicle. They were driving like wild men."

"You probably chased them off a still," John said matter-of-factly.

"You're kidding!"

"Naw, that's the typical reaction of someone hauling moonshine," John replied. "Can you find the place where you saw them loading the truck?"

"You bet!"

That night John and Jim parked near the suspected location, walked in and found the distillery.

Jim was on fire, eager to find more stills. That episode led to a new era in surveillance techniques for ATF and later for other law enforcement agencies. I was lucky enough to get in on it at the beginning.

2.
PANHANDLE REVISITED

THE PANHANDLE SECTION of Clayton County, Georgia was occupied primarily by the Hill clan and well-known for moonshining. Four brothers and several nephews lived in the small community, and most of them were actively engaged in making whiskey.

In September of 1962, ATF Agent Gene Howell was beaten unmercifully as he attempted to arrest three of these notorious moonshiners fleeing an illegal still. Although he managed to shoot all three, Howell later died from his injuries. The Hills survived. Prior to this, Belford Hill had been convicted for possessing and operating a large illegal distillery and for assault on ATF agents Jimmy Satterfield and Earl Lucas. The Hills had little respect for any law enforcement officer, especially ATF agents, who were a constant thorn in their side.

In early January of 1965, Jim Daniels continued his aerial sweep of the Panhandle section, working at all hours and checking the area each time he returned from some other location. His persistence paid off about mid-month. He spotted a faint glow one night in the middle of a hundred-acre swamp, surrounded on all sides by land owned by the Hill clan.

Daniels and I returned to the area several days later in a Cessna 150. We climbed to 10,000 feet, and as he put the trainer into a steep bank the wide expanse of swampland stretched below me.

"Do you see it?" Jim asked.

Straining my eyes, I could see nothing but trees and water.

"Not yet. Where should I look?"

Laughing, Jim rolled the plane back upright and began a wide sweeping turn.

"Over there is where the altercation between Howell and the Hills took place." I recognized the pasture immediately because I had made aerial photographs of the area for use in prosecuting the case.

"I know where I am—but where is the still?" I asked impatiently.

"Okay, draw an imaginary line from the gate they ran through, to our location now. Now look along that line to the center of the swamp. See it?"

We continued to circle. The angle of the Sun on the swamp changed and I could see the faint outline of a rectangular structure. Only from this angle were the straight lines of the camouflaged platform visible.

"Do you think that's a still?" Jim asked.

"Well, it could be a duck blind." I grinned.

Jim and I both knew that this was an active still and that it belonged to the Hills. No one else would dare put a distillery in their territory.

I noticed a small field road running from the rear of Belford's residence to a tiny homemade dock at the edge of the swamp. A pile of brush near the water caught my eye. It didn't look natural. Using binoculars I could make out the end of a flat bottom boat hidden under the brush. Why would Belford want to hide his boat when the only access to it was through his own yard?

This had to be a still, and it was being worked by boat. It would be tough to check out.

"We've been here long enough. Let's head for home."

The next day I called my old friend, Jimmy Satterfield.

"I think we have the Hills located and it looks like another hairy situation."

Jimmy was eager. "Great!" he said. "Can you come over to our office? I'll get M.L. Goodwin and we can meet with Mr. Lane."

Bob Lane was Special Agent in Charge of the Georgia District Office, and M.L. Goodwin was Area Supervisor.

The ATF regional office where I worked was on Peachtree Street in downtown Atlanta. The district office was in the Buckhead section of north Atlanta. It took me 15 minutes to get there and when I walked in, I received the usual cheery greeting from Frankie Waites. One of the unforgettable, dedicated women of ATF, Frankie had been with the outfit since graduating from high school and had attained the position of secretary to the Special Agent in Charge.

Secretaries of SAC's in ATF were usually the ramrods of office activities, the way first sergeants are in the Army. I met Frankie shortly after joining

ATF in 1954, and we became friends immediately. She later married one of the best ATF agents in the country, Ray Hahn. Ray is my kind of guy. He and Frankie are still my close friends.

"What are you doing these days?" Frankie asked cheerfully.

"Still after the Hills," was my reply.

Her expression changed. She knew of our previous run-ins with this lawless bunch and was immediately concerned. "Just be careful, Charley," she said.

Bob Lane motioned for me to come into his office. "Frankie, call downstairs and tell M.L. and Jimmy to come on up. Sit down, Charley."

Lane looked more like a banker than an ATF agent. He had moved up through the ranks to Special Agent in Charge of all ATF agents assigned to the state of Georgia.

"I understand you have the Hills located again," Lane ventured.

"Well, I hope so," I replied.

About that time, Satterfield and Goodwin came in and I began my story. Jim Daniels' existence was still top secret and I skirted the matter by saying, "John Guy's informant showed me an area yesterday that looks awfully good. I think the Hills are back up."

"Where?" Goodwin asked.

"In the big swamp between Belford, Fulton, and Rob's houses."

"Damn. That must cover 200 acres," Jimmy muttered.

"Right! But I know exactly where it is. It's not going to be easy to check," I continued.

"Nothing involving the Hills is ever easy," Lane commented.

"Jimmy, if you and M.L. can break loose from your paperwork this afternoon, I'll get a plane and we can look at it from the air," I suggested.

"I've got to be in Newnan this afternoon but Jimmy can go with you and brief me tomorrow," said M.L.

"Let's go!" Satterfield exclaimed, pushing his chair back.

"Good luck and be careful," Lane said as we left his office.

I made a quick telephone call to Gunn Airfield near Lithonia, east of Atlanta. A Cessna 150 would be ready by the time we arrived. After a stop at Harold's Barbecue on Ridge Avenue we were ready for just about anything.

As we took off, I called Atlanta Hartsfield Approach Control on the aircraft radio and identified myself, requesting clearance through the busy terminal area. I had worked with the local air traffic controllers several times before and they were familiar with my voice. They knew we were engaged in law enforcement work.

"5347 Uniform, radar contact. Maintain present heading of one-nine-zero at 3,000 feet. Confirm you are at 3,000." The controller's instructions were brief and to the point.

"Roger, 47 Uniform heading one-nine-zero, maintaining three."

With that we received clearance through some of the busiest air traffic in the world. For the next ten years I flew hundreds of surveillance missions in highly congested airport traffic in all areas of the eastern U.S., always with excellent cooperation from the FAA air traffic controllers. Once they became aware of our mission and that we were federal law enforcement agents, they were cooperative, courteous and helpful in every way possible. As our activities increased and other agencies began using aircraft for surveillance work, we were issued a code name to identify us to the controllers when we called in.

After clearing the Atlanta Airport control area I began a steady climb to 8,000 feet. We were soon over Hill territory and Satterfield recognized it immediately.

"Jimmy, do you see Belford's house?" I asked. In a short time we had pinpointed the large distillery in the swamp and Satterfield was making mental notes on the best way to walk in without being seen.

"We're going to need some hip boots—that's for sure," he mused.

After Jimmy was satisfied as to the location and best method of approach, we headed back to Gunn Airfield.

"She's all yours, Jimmy, but I'd like to be in on the raid if at all possible."

Jimmy was deep in thought.

"Call me when you know something," I persisted.

"Oh, yeah, sure—this should be interesting!" he said.

The following week Satterfield called to bring me up to date on the Hill investigation.

"I went in with Wilbur Porter and M.L. Goodwin and checked that swamp location. We had to wade through freezing swamp water up to our armpits to get to it. They've built a 1,200 gallon groundhog still on a platform in the middle of the swamp. They cut off trees two feet above the water and built a 15 by 30 foot platform on the stumps. The still has a brick firebox built around it and they're working it with a boat as we suspected.

"It will probably run next week. I'll let you know when we're going to raid if you'd like to go," he added.

"I'd *love* to go."

Surveillance began on Sunday, January 24. On Tuesday, ATF agents M.L. Goodwin, George Tumlin and Frank Kendall and state agent Bob Eckard raided the distillery. Meanwhile, I received a radio call that the raid was imminent and moved my government car into place to block the driveway from Belford's home in case anyone tried to escape from the residence in a vehicle.

"Six-seventy, come on in to the house—Belford's wife just drove a Jeep from the boat landing and she's headed your way. Seize the Jeep," came the radio call.

As I turned into the driveway, the adrenalin started pumping. Reaching the back yard, I saw a Jeep parked in an open shed. I blocked it in with my car. The hood of the Jeep was hot—this was the vehicle.

In a few minutes, Bob Eckard came into the yard.

"We arrested Rob Hill at the boat landing. Belford jumped out of the boat and tried to escape through the swamp. M.L. and I had to fight him to get things under control."

Having known Bob Eckard for some time, I figured he was understating the violence of the moment, but I didn't need to know everything that happened.

I found out later that Belford and Rob had been jumped as they pulled the boatload of liquor into the landing. Belford plunged into the icy water and began to fight with M.L. and Eckard. As M.L. swung to hit Belford with his pistol it slipped out of his hand. Eckard caught the pistol just as it hit the water, saving us a lot of searching and paperwork. Although Belford was as strong as an ox, M.L. and Eckard were certainly a match for him. After they ducked him a time or two in the muddy water he decided to give up.

Satterfield arrived at Belford's house and was briefed on what had taken place. "Where's the key to the Jeep?" he asked.

"I was the first one in the yard and it wasn't in the switch when I got here," I told him.

By this time, M.L. Goodwin and George Tumlin had joined us, leaving Belford and Rob Hill in custody of the other agents who were destroying the distillery.

"I'll go get the key from Mrs. Hill," Jimmy volunteered.

The Hill family home was a typical wood frame farmhouse with a screened-in back porch. When Satterfield reached the back door, Mrs. Hill appeared.

"What in the hell do you want, Satterfield?" she shouted.

"We're going to seize that Jeep for violation of federal law and I want the key," Jimmy answered.

Mrs. Hill disappeared into the house and I thought, Boy, that was easy! But was I ever wrong. She reappeared, this time with a .30-06 deer rifle pointed at the center of Satterfield's stomach. She pulled the bolt back and slammed a cartridge into the chamber, cursing Satterfield at the same time. There were two small, frightened children with her, one on each side.

"Mrs. Hill, you shouldn't be acting like this—think about your children there with you," I pleaded.

"Satterfield's got kids, too," she shrieked. "And I know where he lives."

"Get out of the way, Jimmy!" Bob Eckard shouted. I looked in his direction. Eckard's .357 magnum pistol was pointed at Mrs. Hill and he was in a crouched position, ready to fire.

My mind was racing. I could see the newspaper headlines—"Federal Agents Shoot Mother of Two on Her Back Porch in Presence of Children."

Satterfield stood his ground. Slowly turning his head, he told Eckard, "Let's don't do anything rash!"

Mrs. Hill was still cursing. Satterfield made his way very slowly down the steps to where we were standing.

"We'll get the Jeep if we have to hot-wire it," I told him.

Darkness was fast approaching. I pulled my government Ford into position so the headlights would shine on the back door. When the other officers brought Belford and Rob into the yard, M.L. spoke to Belford.

"We're going to seize the Jeep. Tell your wife to give us the key and it will keep us from arresting her, too."

He did, and still cursing, Mrs. Hill threw the keys into the yard. Thus ended a very tense standoff, and we were all glad to be on our way.

"Hell hath no fury like a woman's wrath."

About a week later, M.L. was surprised to see Mrs. Hill being shown into his office in Atlanta.

"I want to know how to get that Jeep back," she said firmly, getting right to the point.

"You'll have to file a claim and all the necessary papers," M.L. told her, showing her into the office of Assistant Special Agent in Charge Bill Richardson.

As Goodwin left, he heard Mrs. Hill comment, "That's the red-headed son of a bitch who told me to get my ass back to the house."

M.L., having been called worse things in his long law enforcement career, just grinned and kept walking.

3.

KEROSENE BURNERS

ONE COLD MORNING John Guy called.

"Jim Daniels wants us to meet him at Newnan," he said.

By seven o'clock that night, we had located and checked three large distilleries in Haralson and Carroll counties. We returned to Newnan, got some barbecue at Sprayberry's and briefed M.L. Goodwin and Special Agent John Petre on what we had found.

"That should keep them busy for a while," Guy commented as we left.

The next morning, I was in the air again with Wally Hay on an investigation in Hall County. I was flying almost every day on some kind of mission, either trailing liquor cars or raw materials, or checking prolific distillery locations all over the southeast.

Returning one evening with Hay and Guy from south Georgia, I received a radio call from Carl Koppe. "Can you meet us at the old drive-in south of the Farmer's Market?"

"I've got a better idea—how about the dry dock in Jonesboro in 15 minutes?" Dry dock was a code word we had devised for airport.

"Good enough," came Koppe's reply.

About nine o'clock that night I made my approach to the Jonesboro airport. My mind went back to the 1930's and 40's when I was growing up in Jonesboro. None of my school friends knew anything of the dangers I encountered on a daily basis and I knew very little about their lives. We all live in our own worlds and it's very hard to understand what law enforcement involves unless you're a part of it.

SKEECH—the Cessna 172 touched down on the runway and I came back to reality. I found a place to park and we met Koppe and Jim West.

"We've got a truckload of sugar we think will move out sometime tonight. It's parked at the Farmer's Market. We put a beeper (small radio transmitter) on it just after dark but as usual the range is short. Can you help us with the plane?"

One of the great things about working as a federal agent for ATF was that we made our own on-the-spot decisions. The supervisors had come up through the ranks as agents themselves and knew that this freedom was essential to getting the job done.

"Let me get some fuel for the plane and I'll be ready," I replied.

Hay and West left to get some hamburgers while Koppe, Guy and I worked to attach the makeshift radio antenna onto the landing gear strut. The receiver used to pick up the signal from the beeper attached to the suspect vehicle was not exactly state-of-the-art surveillance equipment. It was a variable tuner with a switch for short, medium and long range reception. The only reception you could get on the ground was short, even when it was set to long range.

We wolfed down a couple of greasy spoon hamburgers and were ready to go.

Hay and Koppe would go with me in the plane, and Guy and West would help trail on the ground once the truck started moving.

At 10:15 P.M. Guy called on the radio. "He's moving—looks like he's heading north."

In five minutes we were airborne and checking in with Atlanta International Radar. Soon we were less than a mile from the active runway where incoming traffic was picking up.

"Maintain 1,500 feet MSL and I'll keep you under the incoming traffic," the radar controller said matter-of-factly. "Advise any change of course."

"Roger." We flew just off the end of the two main runways at Atlanta, 27R and 27L. The landing lights of DC-9's and 727's were lined up to the east and coming straight at us. I hoped 1,500 feet was low enough. SWOOSH—a Boeing 727 passed overhead so close we could smell the jet fuel. The smell reminded me of the old kerosene stove my mother cooked on when I was a child. In a few minutes we cleared the incoming traffic and continued to trail the truck north into downtown Atlanta.

We passed through the city without incident and were soon north of the Atlanta metro area, where the air space and ground traffic were far less congested. Guy and West fell back a couple of miles as we trailed the truck visually from the plane.

"Hold up where you are," Wally Hay advised them on the government radio. "He's pulling over onto the shoulder of the road."

With that I immediately switched off all lights on the plane and began a shallow turn away from the truck.

"He's just sitting there," Wally reported to the ground unit. This was a favorite tactic of moonshiners. They would pull over, stop their vehicles and get out and check the tires or just sit and look at every vehicle that passed to see if they were being trailed. They usually did so just after they rounded a curve or passed over a hill so that the trailing vehicle wouldn't see them stop and would have to pass.

"He's moving again!" Koppe broke the silence. We had been airborne for about two hours and it was past midnight as we reached the farming area around Maysville and Gillsville on the Banks-Jackson County line. Everything below was pitch black except for an occasional booger light at a few farm houses. (These are outside lights that come on automatically at sundown and keep the boogers away.)

"He just turned his lights off," Koppe commented. My hand went to the aircraft light switches once more and I eased the throttle back to reduce the sound of our engine. We flew at 5,000 feet and off to one side of the truck in a very shallow turn.

"You still got him?" I asked. "I've got the spot where his lights went out."

I began tuning the airplane's navigational radios to directional stations nearby. In two minutes I had our location pinpointed as closely as possible.

Koppe was peering through heavy binoculars. "He's pulled into a barn at the rear of a farmhouse. We'd better get out of here."

Gently I completed my turn and headed toward the airport beacon in Gainesville.

Guy and West met us at the dry dock and we filled them in on what we had seen. The next morning James Stratigos, Resident Agent in Charge of the Gainesville Post of Duty, flew with us to the area, this time at a very high altitude. Using the coordinates I had secured the night before, I found the general location. After a couple of minutes Koppe spotted the farm and barn. Stratigos knew the county well and assured us he could find it on the ground. With that we dropped him off at the Gainesville airport and returned to Atlanta. It was his baby now, and we knew it was in good hands.

The use of airplanes to trail ground vehicles was an entirely new technique. Aircraft had been used for years to look for illicit distilleries but to my knowledge, no one had ever tried to trail ground vehicles with aircraft, especially at night. Jim Daniels and ATF pioneered what was later to become a primary weapon in the war on crime.

To this day most people find it hard to believe that back in the early sixties we were leading the way. One reason we were successful for many years was that we never divulged our secret weapon. Neither the pilot nor any observer ever appeared as witnesses in court. The only evidence used in case reports was that obtained by the ground units. This became a bone of contention on several occasions when ATF agents wanted to use testimony from airborne agents to strengthen their case against liquor law violators, but supervisors like Bill Griffin refused, sticking to their guns in order to protect the secrecy of our project.

A week or so later, the distillery was seized and destroyed by local officers. No one was arrested. This happened frequently in areas of the southeast where distrust between federal and state officers prevented a close working relationship. At least they didn't know how we had found it.

4.

ICY TRAIL

THE FIRST DAY of February was icy cold with sleet and freezing rain. The roads in the Atlanta area were almost impassible. With the help of mud and snow tires on my government car, I was able to get to the office around noontime. Regional Special Group Supervisor Gene Hart called John Guy, Wally Hay and me into his office.

"We've received a call from Alabama agents that a tractor-trailer load of moonshine is headed toward Atlanta from the Mobile area. Can you give them some assistance?"

I had heard that ATF agents had located a gigantic illicit distillery somewhere in the Mobile or Gulfport, Mississippi area but I never guessed the moonshiners would be hauling tractor-trailer loads as far north as Atlanta.

"Well, flying is out of the question for now, the weather is so bad, but we'll try to help on the ground," I replied.

"Good luck and be careful," Gene said.

We barreled out of Atlanta on Highway 78 and arrived in Anniston, Alabama about seven that evening. At ten o'clock we learned that the truck was headed north toward Rome, Georgia. I returned to Atlanta around midnight to try to get some sleep while John and Wally kept the truck under observation in Rome. By seven the next morning the weather had cleared, although it was still very cold. I called Deputy Ed Michaels, one of the best aerial observers I ever worked with.

"Can you meet me at Gunn Airfield? It looks like this could be a long one."

"Sure thing," he replied.

Mike and I flew to Chattanooga, some 60 miles north of Rome, and waited. The tractor-trailer had moved to LaFayette, Georgia, but had encountered icy roads and stopped at a truck stop.

One of the true legends of east Tennessee, Special Agent Roy Tubb, met us at the airport and we spent a cold night in his government car. At 5:30 A.M. the government radio broke the silence.

"He's moving north toward Chattanooga."

Grabbing our military surplus arctic coats, we headed to the Cessna 172.

"I hope this thing will start in this bitter cold. Keep your fingers crossed," I mused aloud.

I double-checked the controls and pulled the propeller through by hand until I could feel the oil begin to loosen up. I climbed in and primed the engine with raw gasoline until it was running out on the ground. I realized the fire hazard involved, but I hoped that when the engine fired it would keep running the first time. The starter groaned for about 30 seconds before the engine caught. I didn't let it die.

In a short time we were off the ground and headed south. By this time the truck was almost to Chattanooga, and we had no difficulty picking him up. The longest aerial surveillance job we had ever undertaken was about to begin.

The Cessna 172 is a four place general aviation aircraft, one of the best airplanes ever built. It's not fast but is a pleasure to fly. As we zeroed in on the truck, the sun was just beginning to come up. The ground was covered with ice and snow and although the temperature was hovering around 16° F, we were comfortable in our big coats and enjoying the view.

"We've got him," Tubb reported to the ground units.

"Ten-four. We're falling back a couple of miles—keep us posted," Wally replied.

The road conditions made the driving tough. There were numerous patches of ice. In several locations tractor-trailers had jackknifed and slid off the road the night before, and the going was extremely slow. Five hours of slow flight later, the truck had only gone as far as Bristol, Tennessee and we were running low on fuel.

The truck driver must have been tired and hungry by this time, because just as I was about to make a decision as to how much longer we could fly, he pulled into a truck stop south of the Tri-Cities Airport. We advised the ground units we were pulling off, then I contacted Approach Control Radar.

"Tri-Cities Approach—this is Cessna 7397 Golf—five miles south, landing Tri-Cities."

"Roger, 7397 Golf—squawk 4323 and ident. Contact Tri-Cities Tower on 119.5."

When the airport tower controller answered my call, his first question was, "Say type aircraft?"

"Cessna 172," I replied.

There was a long pause, then "We have almost 18 inches of snow and the only runway cleared is two-three. The wind is from 310 at 20 knots, gusting to 30 knots."

"Roger, understand," I said without thinking.

"Enter left downwind for two-three—report airport in sight."

"This is going to be hairy," I commented to Tubb and Michaels.

"You can make it," Mike assured me. We had flown together many times before, night and day, but I knew that landing a light aircraft like the 172 in a 25 knot crosswind was not going to be a picnic.

"97 Golf, follow the Eastern Electra on long final— do you have him in sight?"

"Roger," I replied.

Total concentration is required in landing an airplane, especially in a gusting crosswind. I had slowed to an approach speed of 70, and when we turned final we began to feel the effects of the wind gusts. I tightened my seat belt and told my passengers to stow anything loose in the cabin and get ready for a rough ride.

We followed the Electra, a large four-engine turbo prop airliner. The pilot had to maintain an extreme crab angle in order to keep the plane headed toward the runway.

The wind was from our right, so in order to keep the plane from drifting to the left, I held the right wing down—way down—and used left rudder to maintain my heading toward the runway. This cross controlling is one of the most difficult maneuvers to master while learning to fly. I had only been flying for about a year, but my instructors were two of the best in the business, Jim Daniels and Ken Sallies. I had logged a lot of hours flying in difficult circumstances and didn't have sense enough to be afraid.

The Electra was about to touch down. His right wing was so low I thought it would hit the snow banked along the edge of the runway. Then the right main landing gear touched and I was fascinated by how the pilot kept the wing down and continued on one wheel until his speed dissipated and he was able to get the left gear and nose wheel on the runway.

Well, if that's the way the experts do it, that's the way I'll do it, I thought.

"97 Golf, cleared to land—wind 310 at 22, gusting to 26."

I quickly tapped the mike button between bumps. With my left hand, I had the wheel of the 172 turned all the way to the right while holding hard left rudder with my feet and adjusting the throttle with my right hand. I didn't have time to talk.

I was as amazed as everyone else how well the landing was accomplished.

"97 Golf, nice going. Taxi to the ramp." I thought I heard a little relief in the controller's voice. He probably detected some in mine as I replied, "Roger."

While the airplane was being serviced, Michaels, Tubb and I ate a couple of hamburgers. Wally Hay found us in the coffee shop.

"Who's that hoople?" Wally asked in his typical energetic, abrupt New York manner upon seeing Roy Tubb. Roy was wearing his usual still-raiding clothes—an old army field jacket, corduroy pants and paratrooper boots that looked as though they had been through both World Wars. He also had such a heavy beard that ten minutes after shaving he sported a dark five o'clock shadow.

"Roy's one of the best ATF field agents in Tennessee," I answered. Looks can be deceiving.

In less than 30 minutes we were back in the air. The ground unit advised us of the truck's location, and in no time we found him.

By this time he was in Virginia. Although as federal agents our authority was not limited by state lines, there was an unwritten rule that any time we were working in another region the proper thing to do was notify the local ATF agents.

"Better try to get in touch with the Roanoke Post of Duty," I called on the ATF frequency to John Guy. Before Guy could answer, a new voice came on the air.

"We've been listening to you for the past two hours. You must be in Roanoke." A strong radio signal usually meant close proximity to the unit receiving the transmission, but the signal from an airplane was ten times normal.

"We'll explain later," I advised. "We've got a vehicle heading north and it looks like he'll be in your area shortly. Where is a good place to meet one of our units?"

The Virginia agents caught on quickly and arranged a meeting place, keeping radio traffic to a minimum.

By 6:00 P.M. we had been following the truck and slow flying for nearly 12 hours. I was completely exhausted.

"John, we're going to have to quit at Lynchburg. I've had it."

Wally Hay broke in—"I'll try to get a pilot and plane in Lynchburg—hold on for a little longer."

"Okay," I grunted.

It was beginning to get dark when we landed at Lynchburg. We were advised to taxi to the Texaco ramp, and Wally was waiting there with a plane and pilot. Quickly we transferred the beeper receiver with the attendant antenna and wire to the other plane and in ten minutes Wally and the ex-Marine pilot were in the air. Ed Michaels and I took Wally's car and Roy Tubb went with John Guy. We became one of the ground units. In addition to two ground vehicles from the southeast region, there were probably six cars from the mid-Atlantic region, and every time we passed through a different post of duty we picked up at least one more car to add to the caravan trailing the truck.

At midnight we reached Richmond, where the truck turned back south.

"He's onto us," I told Mike.

"He's got to be with all those cars lined up behind him," agreed Michaels.

I had been flying or driving for 18 hours straight. I saw a Holiday Inn sign and pulled in. "We're going off duty at the Holiday Inn just south of Richmond," I told anyone listening and turned off the radio before they could answer.

The motel was remodeling and there was only one room available. Luckily, it had two beds. We had just dozed off when someone pounded on the door. Sleepily I opened it to find Wally standing there with his only luggage—a huge pair of military surplus binoculars and the cumbersome beeper radio receiver with ten feet of wire and wire antennas wadded up under his arm.

I burst out laughing. I still wonder what the hotel clerk thought when this guy with his white shirttail half out and all the funny looking gear under his arm staggered into the lobby and asked for a room. Despite his looks, Wally had persuaded the clerk to put a rollaway bed in our room. He talked a mile a minute, keeping me in stitches.

"That ex-Marine pilot went to sleep a couple of times and I had to keep waking him up so we'd be headed in the right direction. There were so many ground units following the truck there was no way they could lose him, so I decided to quit for the night. It's a good thing I heard you sign off here."

Wally finally settled down and we did get some sleep, but not much.

The next morning when we checked in we were told that the truck was approaching Raleigh, N.C. "We'll pick up our airplane at Lynchburg and head toward Raleigh," I muttered to no one in particular. With that, we let the hammer down on the Pontiac and arrived in Lynchburg in no time flat.

Wally took his government car and Michaels and I took off for Raleigh in the plane. Wally was to catch up with us there as soon as he could. Special Agents Joe Carter and D.C. Lawson met us at the airport.

"You two look like you could use some rest," Joe observed. "We've got enough people on the truck to let us know if he moves."

Gratefully, Mike and I checked into the Heart of Raleigh motel and it was the next morning before I was aware of anything. After more than 12 hours of continuous slow flying I was whipped.

At 6:00 A.M., Carter pounded on the door. "Open up—he's moving!"

Michaels and I both hit the door at the same time. By the time we reached the airport the ground units were calling to say that the truck had only moved across town to another truck stop. We spent another day and night on observation of the truck and then on Saturday evening—four days after first picking him up south of Chattanooga and trailing him for more than 1,000 miles—we decided that the driver had abandoned the tractor-trailer. We seized the truck and 2,840 gallons of moonshine whiskey at eleven that night. The driver, Dewey Doris, was arrested later as he came out of the truck stop bunkhouse.

The North Carolina agents were pleased because it gave them an excellent month production-wise. The Alabama agents could have seized the truck in Alabama and the Tennessee agents, in Tennessee. The Virginia agents almost cried when the truck crossed the line back into North Carolina, but we all worked together and had a good time.

Sunday was spent checking the truck and its contents for evidence and fingerprints. On Monday, I met with D.C. Lawson and Joe Carter about the case report, then headed back to Atlanta in marginal flying weather. I spent the rest of the week working in the regional office trying to get over the past seven days. My wife Dot was pleased that I was home for a change.

Sheriff Pink Allen and ATF Agents Jimmy Satterfield and Doug Denney at large groundhog still, Haralson County, Georgia.

5.

QUICK DRAW

CHATTANOOGA, TENNESSEE HAD the reputation of being a haven for car thieves, safecrackers, moonshiners and all other criminal types. Its location on the Tennessee River a short distance from the Georgia-Alabama line made it ideal for thieves. Criminals operated out of Chattanooga across the state lines, either to escape Tennessee authorities or to commit crimes in Georgia or Alabama and return to the relative safety of Chattanooga.

In 1959 and '60 I worked as an undercover operative in a very dangerous and extensive investigation in the Chattanooga area. Now five years later the Chief of Special Investigations, Marvin Shaw was sending me once again into one of the most lawless cities in the South.

"Charley, I'm going to give you all the men you need to do the job." Shaw was serious. "Primarily you'll be working on the major violators in the Chattanooga area, but you know you're not limited in any way. If the trail leads into other areas—or other states—go to it. Call Howard Ledford, the RAC (Resident Agent in Charge) and he'll meet with you and agents Joe Powell and Charlie Riddle. Let me know if you need any more help."

Thus began an investigation that lasted more than five months and required my coordinating the activities of twelve special agents. We rented two large two-bedroom apartments on Lake Chickamauga and worked 12-hour shifts out of this location.

The operation started with Ledford, Powell, Riddle and me. Soon we were joined by Bud Keathley, Riley Oxley, Buddy Trickey, Stan Frye, Jerome von Tempske, Paul Underwood, Jim Berry and Roy Tubb. Laverne Hoover and Harry Braxton also assisted from the Rome, Georgia office.

One of our first moves was to rent a Cessna 172 and survey suspected moonshining areas in Signal Mountain, Montlake, Chickamauga Gulch and Soddy Daisy. Ledford came up with an informer who told us that Sam Nichols and Bobby Henry were being furnished large amounts of moonshine by people in the Soddy-Daisy area north of Chattanooga.

Early one Saturday morning the informer, a former Chattanooga police officer, showed me areas of suspected moonshine activity in Hamilton, Sequachie and Bledsoe counties. With this much information, I felt sure we could make a dent in moonshining in that area.

A few days later, Ledford and I dropped Riddle and Powell out near a reported liquor stash location in the Montlake section of Walden's Ridge.

"This is Henry Hayden Territory—be careful," Ledford warned as the two other agents slid quickly out of the car. "We'll give you three hours to check it and pick you up at about nine tonight."

When we picked up Riddle and Powell they both were excited.

"We found two active stills and could hear stills running all over the ridge. This is going to be fun!" Riddle exclaimed.

Within a period of three weeks our group found nine separate illegal distilleries in a five square mile area on Walden's Ridge, a high plateau comprised of several hundred acres overlooking the rugged country north of Chattanooga. There are only two or three roads to the top, and any strange vehicle immediately becomes suspect to the residents. Most of the houses are built in the shotgun style and feature at least two dogs and one dilapidated vehicle in the yard. The people are clannish and independent except when it comes to receiving welfare checks and food stamps, which admittedly, some of them desperately need. The making of moonshine was merely a supplemental source of income for most of them.

When one of our agents asked a small boy living in the area what he wanted to do when he grew up, he replied matter-of-factly, "I'm going to draw."

"That's great," replied the agent, thinking that he meant he would be an artist. "What are you going to draw?"

"A check from the government," was the quick reply.

A humorous but sad situation. Welfare does indeed perpetuate itself.

Within the next three weeks, we developed a routine of work. At two in the morning one of us would drop two or more agents off on top of the escarpment to check the previously located distilleries. If a distillery was in operation, the agents would observe it and gather evidence; if not, they searched for new illegal stills.

At two o'clock the following morning more agents would be dropped out and the first ones picked up. The distilleries were small, averaging about 1,500 gallons of mash and producing about 200 gallons of moonshine twice a week, but they operated on a regular schedule.

Four of them were in the immediate area of Henry Hayden's residence and another one was only 200 yards from the rear of the home of Henry's brother Benton.

We also kept a large whiskey transfer point under surveillance. After confirming that moonshine was being loaded out of an outbuilding onto vehicles which would then head toward Chattanooga, we decided to use an airplane to trail the vehicles into the city.

Ledford and I were on standby at the Chattanooga Airport when the call came in. "He's loading."

"We're on the way," I responded into the microphone of the government radio as we ran toward the airplane. I received immediate clearance from the tower to taxi to the closest runway and take off. In five minutes we were heading north and gaining altitude, the Cessna 172 straining in the cool spring air.

"It looks like he's finished loading. It's an old model black Chevrolet pickup truck. He's got about 150 gallons on it," Riley Oxley whispered.

Damn, he must be close by, I thought.

When we reached the stash location, Ledford quickly pointed it out. "We've got the vehicle—looks like he's just coming out of the drive," he reported to Oxley.

Two clicks on the radio and our message was confirmed.

Chattanooga is surrounded by mountains and ridges—Lookout Mountain, Signal Mountain, Missionary Ridge and Walden's Ridge—and while the city is about 700 feet above sea level, the surrounding area rises up to 2,500 feet. The liquor truck was headed down off this plateau toward Chattanooga. Keeping him in sight from the plane meant that we had to fly below the tops of the plateaus and mountains at times.

Ledford was in radio contact with Roy Tubb and Charlie Riddle, who were in a ground unit. "Where are you?" he asked.

"Just south of the spot where we caught Don Frice."

"Okay, I see you. Pull into that next driveway and wait—he's almost to your location."

As the truck passed Riddle's parked car, it sped up. Thus began a long, wild chase with the federal agents attempting to stop the liquor truck over a distance of 25 miles. From our front row seat in the airplane we kept them advised of potential road hazards and the movements of the truck. The chase ended on top of another mountain when the truck left the road and went over an embankment. Riddle caught the driver, Ernest Speer a short distance from the truck, arrested him and charged him with possession of 125 gallons of moonshine.

Two days later, Riddle and I had just finished breakfast at a greasy spoon diner at the base of Signal

Mountain when we got a call from Howard Ledford from the top of the mountain.

"A '58 blue and white Plymouth just left here headed toward Chattanooga with a load of liquor."

I floorboarded the '60 Chrysler V-8 and in about five minutes we reached the intersection of the "W" road and Highway 127. Precisely at nine o'clock the Plymouth passed us, headed toward Chattanooga. We came up on his back bumper before he knew it and he quickly turned into a side road and poured on the coal. There was no way he could outrun the Chrysler. When he hit a ditch trying to make a curve he bailed out on foot. Riddle quickly caught Gene Denton and I checked the Plymouth. It contained 120 gallons of moonshine in six-gallon cola drums.

By this point in my career I had worked in every state in the southeast but I never ceased to be amazed at the variety of containers used by moonshiners to transport liquor and the many different types of stills used to make the stuff. The methods of production and transportation of moonshine varied from state to state, and even from section to section within a state. The only place I saw moonshine transported in these six-gallon cola drums was around Chattanooga. In other areas they used everything from five-gallon demijohn and GI cans to one-gallon glass and plastic jugs, half-gallon jars and one-gallon tin cans. On one occasion we seized several hundred gallons in half-gallon plastic containers.

The distilleries also varied, including 200 to 2,000 gallon ground hog fermenter stills, upright steam boiler distilleries, coffin or pan type 800 to 1,200

gallon steel tank fermenter stills, silver cloud galva-
nized stills and, only occasionally, a small copper pot
still. I have found illegal distilleries in the basements
and attics of very expensive houses as well as in
barns, chicken houses, specially-constructed underground locations, forests and farmland and large
metropolitan areas.

The moonshiners used improvisation and a pio-
neering spirit in their lawless operations. The ATF
agent also had to call upon his ingenuity and improvisation most of the time to apprehend them. It was an
exciting and challenging job.

After months of surveillance interrupted by several weeks of work on other active investigations and
attendance in federal court, we made our round-up
the first week in June. Twenty-two stills were seized
and destroyed, seven vehicles and a large amount of
sugar were seized and nine men arrested.

It was estimated that during the period of operation these distilleries produced 13,000 gallons of
moonshine whiskey.

The moonshiners were convicted and received
sentences ranging from three years hard time to
probation. For a while things slowed down on Walden's
Ridge—but not for long.

ATF Agent Von Tempske at groundhog type still, Chickamauga Gulch, Tennessee.

6.

MOVE OVER!

BY JUNE OF 1965 Jim Daniels, the airline captain turned investigator, was really rolling. Much of his off-duty time was spent flying Cessna 150's and looking for illegal distilleries. During that summer we checked and raided stills in Paulding, Haralson, DeKalb, Douglas, Carroll and Barrow counties.

In mid-July Daniels located a large distillery about three miles northwest of Buchanan, Georgia. John Guy dropped Special Agent John Kreeger and me off a mile or so from the location and we walked in, reaching the still in late afternoon. As soon as we hit the vehicle sign (fresh tracks) I knew this was an active still.

I whispered to John, "Daniels is right again!"

Kreeger was on my heels all the way. The temperature was in the high 90's. We had walked over a mile now through some rough territory but all of a sudden, I was no longer tired. The adrenalin had started to work and I became alert to every sound and movement. Moving quietly, we rounded a bend in the still road and slipped into the still yard.

I stopped so quickly that Kreeger ran into me.

"Sorry," he mumbled.

No one was at the distillery but we carefully checked it, being sure to stay out of any soft earth where we might leave tracks.

I told Kreeger, "They've apparently just finished running the liquor. There's about 350 gallons here and it's still warm."

Steam rose from the 2,000-gallon fermenter still. We backed off about 200 yards into the woods.

"670 to 585," I called to John Guy on a small portable government FM radio.

"585," came the answer.

"This thing is active. Kreeger and I are going to stay close in case they come back in."

"Ten-four. If you'll go back to where I dropped you off, I'll drop someone else to help raid," John replied. "I'll be there in 30 minutes."

It was getting dark fast. I left Kreeger to watch the distillery and took off through the woods. Guy had joined up with agents Joe Burton, Harry Braxton and Emory Sheppard after he left us. When I arrived at the drop-off place, Braxton and Sheppard were waiting for me. We made our way back to the still site.

"We'll surround the place and wait. Kreeger and Sheppard, you cover the back side. Braxton and I will make the initial move if anyone comes in to load the moonshine," I said. Kreeger and Sheppard eased off into the darkness.

Working moonshine stills requires a tremendous amount of patience and persistence. I knew I was in good company for raiding and it wasn't long before I was dozing in the warm summer night.

Shortly after midnight the low whine and groan of an old Ford truck woke me. Braxton was already peering through the darkness in that direction. We began to creep through the undergrowth toward the distillery. Sound travels for miles on a quiet night in a rural area, and it seemed as if the truck might run over us at any minute.

As it passed, I whispered to Braxton, "We'll let him start unloading before we move in."

The truck stopped. All was quiet for about five minutes. The moonshiners were listening for any unusual sounds before they started work. Apparently satisfied they were alone, they began to unload more than a ton of sugar from the truck.

"Okay, let's go," I whispered. I knew that Sheppard and Kreeger would be alert and ready by this time and I was anxious to get my hands on these law violators. Moving quietly in a crouched position, I soon reached the front of the truck. Braxton came around the other side.

"G—damn!" one of the violators shouted in sheer terror.

Braxton grabbed Ray Ford at the truck and I took off after Rob Gleason. It was a short chase and I subdued him quickly. Sheppard and Kreeger burst into the still yard looking in all directions.

"We've already caught both of them."

Disappointment showed on their faces. One of the joys of the job was being able to catch someone at every still.

★ ★ ★

Another of the great joys and advantages of being an ATF agent was meeting and working with officers from all areas of law enforcement, including one-man police forces.

Being stationed in the Atlanta area gave me the opportunity to work with old-time Fulton County Deputies Luther Hardy and his partner Peppers, and others such as Bob Harper from south Fulton County.

Harper called me at home one weekend. "I've got good information that a load of liquor will be coming into the west side early Monday morning. I know where he's supposed to set the liquor off on Simpson Road."

"Okay, how early?"

"About four-thirty."

I didn't mind working all night but getting up at four in the morning was not much fun. I met Harper and his partner, ATF Agent Joe Powell, that Monday morning at 4:30 and we backed into an alley about a block from the Simpson Road location.

ATF had begun to get a little more recognition from the Treasury Department since our active role in quelling the Montgomery Riots. We were even assigned some decent police-type vehicles for use in enforcing the liquor laws. I was driving a 1964 Plymouth with the 402 Hemi engine that was giving race fans a thrill all over the southeast. It would fly.

I was beginning to think that this was going to be another "hummy" when Bob nudged me.

"There he goes."

A nice-looking 1956 Buick had just passed. I fired up the Plymouth. It was just before dawn so I left my lights off and was on his back bumper before he knew it. When my blue light, headlights and siren all came on at the same time he was so startled, he jumped the curb and sideswiped a telephone pole before stopping. The door flew open and a black man hit the ground running. I blocked the Buick in with my Plymouth and told Powell to stay with the car. Harper had already taken off after the liquor hauler and disappeared around the corner of a house.

I loved a foot chase. As Harper later told the story, he heard me coming up behind him, shouting, "Move over!"

I caught Richard Holly after a short chase through a vegetable garden and began to wonder if I had made a mistake in passing Harper. In the struggle with this wild, muscular man I was lifted off my feet a time or two. We weren't doing the vegetables in the garden any good, either. I finally tripped the moonshiner and was about to get him down on the ground when Harper arrived. I was glad to see him. We brought him back to the Buick and found 90 gallons of moonshine in the trunk and back seat.

The early morning run paid off after all.

Trip boy caught delivering liquor in six-gallon cola drums, Chattanooga, Tennessee.

7.

CLOSE CALL

A NIP OF fall was in the air, and it was great flying weather. In mid-October,Deputy Ed Michaels, State Agent Bob Eckard and I trailed several trip cars with the plane in DeKalb, Henry, Jackson, Rockdale and Fulton counties. We gathered enough evidence to seize three vehicles and a total of 151 gallons of moonshine. Robert Lee and Mac Hilliard were arrested.

Later that month, Special Agent Hugh Merrill called.

"Charley, I've got information that J.R. Turner, your old nemesis, and another major liquor law violator named R.L. Lattimer are in partnership on a huge illicit distillery somewhere in Habersham County."

"Great! When do you want to go to work on them?" I asked.

"How about in the morning?"

"I'll be there."

Hugh was stationed in Cornelia at the time and had developed some very good informers. We began by trailing suspected vehicles with the airplane. Many years before, Hugh had taken flying lessons and he was always eager to go along as observer.

After two weeks of surveillance work with Hugh, Wally Hay and Ray Hahn we finally located the still about four miles north of Clarkesville. We trailed a big load of sugar and other materials into a new barn on two occasions, both times late at night.

As Hugh, Wally and I were circling the area at two o'clock one morning, a beam of light hit our airplane from below. Immediately, I cut our running lights and turned away from the area. The beam of light apparently came from an automobile about five miles from the suspected distillery location and we were concerned that someone was suspicious of our plane.

While this was going on other agents were on ground surveillance at the home of Snuffy James, one of J.R.'s partners in Dawson County. Snuffy had been involved in moonshining for many years and was a prime suspect in this operation.

We landed at Toccoa Airport at 3:00 A.M. and Hugh and I caught a couple hours' sleep in the plane. The chill of the fall morning awakened us, cold and hungry. But breakfast would have to wait.

"463 to 670—we've got activity at our location." Bud Hazelip was calling from the James area in Dawson County. Merrill reached for the microphone while I started priming the engine on the cold Cessna 172.

"We're on the way," Hugh answered.

It was just after daybreak but I was now fully awake. I checked the engine gauges on the roll and by the time we got to the end of the runway we were ready to take off.

"Here we go," I told him, pouring the power to the Cessna. Early morning and late afternoon are generally the best times to fly, and early on cold mornings airplanes virtually leap off the ground. It's an exhilarating feeling.

We climbed steadily for about 15 minutes and had reached an altitude of 11,000 feet by the time we arrived in the James area. The less noticeable we were, the better.

"A black one and a half-ton truck just left the house going south," the radio crackled.

"We've got him," Hugh answered without hesitation.

I quickly pulled the airplane up and into a steep turn to the left to keep the truck in sight. One of the agents on the ground said later that we did a Split "S" but I don't think so.

I throttled back and dropped one notch of flaps to slow the plane down to about 55 m.p.h. The occasional beep of the stall warning horn told me we were flying at about the right airspeed. Hugh settled into the back seat directly behind me so both of us could keep the vehicle in sight.

The observer has to keep his eye on the suspected vehicle at all times, advise ground units by radio of its position and give instructions as the trail continues. Trailing in heavy traffic, especially at night, requires that the observer never look away from his vehicle. It is a very demanding and tiring job. The constant concentration, noise and sometimes rough ride make it tough.

The pilot also has a tremendous responsibility in maneuvering the aircraft to keep the vehicle in sight, watching for other aircraft, maintaining contact with FAA controllers, monitoring their many transmissions and also listening with one ear to the ATF ground units, all while in slow flight which itself requires a great deal of concentration. After five hours of constant noise, vibration and stress, many times I could hardly lift my arms to get out of the plane.

As we trailed the truck south toward Atlanta from the James area, Merrill and I were comfortable and enjoying the smooth morning ride when suddenly— ku-chunk—CHUNK–KU-CHUNK—the engine faltered. All pilots develop a keen ear to the sounds of an aircraft engine, and the more you fly the keener it gets. But anyone could tell this engine was about to stop completely.

One of the first things a pilot is taught is that the throat of the airplane's carburetor is subject to forming ice in certain weather conditions. The remedy for this is pulling a cable linkage to divert warm air from around the muffler into the carburetor and shut off cold outside air.

I grabbed the handle and pulled it, closing off the outside air and directing in the warm air. KU-CHUNK—and then silence! I slammed the carburetor air lever back in and got a little response from the engine, but not much.

"We're losing the truck," Hugh said calmly.

"To hell with the truck—I'm going to try to get this thing to Gainesville."

We were flying over the upper reaches of Lake Lanier, a huge body of water more than 30 miles long and several miles wide in places.

"Gainesville Tower, 7397 Golf about 14 northwest—I'm having a little engine problem. I'll be landing Gainesville if we can make it," I called.

"7397 Golf—cleared to land any runway Gainesville. Keep us advised," came the answer.

By this time I had discovered that by using just a small amount of carburetor heat I could keep the engine running, even though it was so rough it was shaking the whole airplane. We had lost altitude at first, but as we continued toward the airport the engine gradually came back to life and we were able to hold our own at 2,500 feet.

"Gainesville, this is 7397 Golf. I have the airport in sight."

"Roger, 97 Golf, cleared to land any runway. What is your situation?"

"The roughness seems to have cleared up. Sorry for the trouble we caused," I replied.

"No trouble. We're glad you made it."

Fire trucks and service vehicles were lined up all along the main runway, lights flashing.

"Looks like they're waiting for us to crash," Hugh said.

"Well, I don't plan to do that. We'll land on this short runway and I'll taxi around behind that maintenance hangar before they can get to us." I was a little embarrassed about causing so much commotion, but I guess it gave the local people some excitement.

A mechanic met us at the plane as soon as we shut it down. We pulled the cowl and he checked the engine. "You probably got some carburetor ice," he said confidently. "I don't see anything wrong."

Thanking him, Hugh and I made our way to the coffee shop and took our time having breakfast while the crowd cleared out.

That night, we met with Bud Hazelip and Agent
Paul Campbell.

"We've seen enough to give us probable cause to
obtain a federal search warrant," Hazelip reported.
"Charley, you and Hugh hit the ground in the morning with Campbell. Ray Hahn, Wally Hay and Billy
Moore will be on standby for any vehicle movement
you report."

"Sounds good," I said.

"We'll be there," chimed in Hugh. "I'd love to tie
J.R. to this one."

Just at daybreak the next day Campbell, Merrill
and I walked into the area and began surveillance of
the barn and farmhouse. I was about 200 yards to the
rear and side of the house, across an open field from
the barn. Campbell was on the other side of the barn.
I could hear the fuel oil burner and knew this had to
be a large steam boiler still.

A few hours later James Winfred, whom I had
arrested before, left the house and went to the barn.
Forty-five minutes later he returned to the house.

At noontime, Paul Campbell called on the radio,
whispering, "Someone just left the house headed
toward the still house." Then, "Two men are walking
back toward the farmhouse in a hurry."

A car started at the house and moved out of the
back yard onto the public road.

"670 to any unit—670 to any unit," I called on the
radio. No answer.

Then, "This is 463—go ahead."

I told Hazelip what had happened. "Bud, I think
we'd better get a federal arrest warrant for Winfred
because I don't think he'll be back."

"Ten-four. Let's get with the others."

We talked it over with the other agents and decided to execute the federal search warrant at two that afternoon. As we suspected, no one was at the farmhouse or the distillery but we seized and destroyed more than 11,000 gallons of mash, a 4,000-gallon steel still and 128 gallons of moonshine.

From the looks of the house, a man, woman and small child were living there, and another man was living upstairs. It wasn't uncommon to find families living in buildings near distilleries, or even in the same building with the still.

I obtained a federal arrest warrant for Winfred the next day and he gave himself up the following week.

Two days later, Hugh Merrill and other agents from the Cornelia post of duty raided a stash house about three miles from the distillery. They seized 884 gallons of moonshine and three pickup trucks, and arrested Jerry Goforth and A.L. Powell. During our aerial surveillance of the distillery location, we had trailed one of these pickups to this same stash house, so the effort panned out.

Most of the time in cases like this we never knew what or who tipped off the violators.

We could only speculate. J.R.'s luck was holding.

Charley Weems and "97 Goober."

8.

SKEETER

ONE MORNING IN early December, 1965, the telephone rang in our squad room.

"Squad room, Weems," I answered.

"Charley, this is Frank Lane. Can you get a plane and meet me at the Athens dry dock at four-thirty this afternoon? I think we've got something good—at least it's a good place to start."

"Okay, but let me check the weather first," I replied.

"I've already checked. It looks good for the next two or three days," came Frank's answer.

Knowing that Lane was an ex-Navy pilot who was certainly qualified to make sound flying decisions, I didn't hesitate.

"I'll be there at 4:30."

Wally Hay, an ATF agent originally from New York City, had been stationed in Atlanta for about a year and we had become friends, working together on several cases in north Georgia. Wally was also interested in flying and was in the process of getting his pilot's license.

"You want to go on a deal this afternoon? I don't know when we'll be back," I asked.

"Sure!" Wally was always ready to go, especially if it involved flying.

At 4:00 P.M. we touched down at the Athens airport. When Frank arrived he suggested we get something to eat, saying, "It'll probably be a long night."

As we drove, Lane filled us in. "We have good information that a big outfit is being supplied raw materials (sugar, containers, and all the necessary ingredients to make moonshine) from a farmhouse in Franklin County. We think they're working it at night and we hope to locate the still by watching the stash house. I know where it is but haven't seen it from the air."

"After we eat we need to get out there before dark so we can get ourselves oriented," I suggested.

Working aerial surveillance at night is extremely difficult under the best of circumstances but we had learned fast and gained more confidence with every success.

The hours of daylight were getting shorter and we had just arrived in the area of the stash location when the booger lights at some of the farms in the area began to come on.

"That's the house at the end of that long drive just off to your right," Frank said.

"Are you sure?" Wally asked.

"Yeah. I know because I can see the old abandoned service station that's just south of that driveway."

"I'm going to climb on up and out several miles. I've got the location pinpointed," I said.

I tuned one navigational radio to receive Norcross VOR (ground directional station) and the other, Athens, in order to get directional bearings off both stations. Where they crossed on the aerial map was our location.

As we continued to climb, I remembered my recent experience with carburetor icing and pulled on the carburetor heat occasionally.

"A vehicle just turned into the driveway and cut his lights—we need to get in closer," Frank said.

Leveling off, I pulled the power back and turned toward the house, at the same time flipping off my running lights. Wally had his binoculars trained on the area.

"It's a pickup truck. He just stopped at the house."

We stayed high and quiet.

In about 30 minutes an automobile came in, also without lights. The truck left, followed shortly by the car. When they hit the main road their lights came on and they turned towards Carnesville.

"I'm going to drop down a little since he's moving. Don't take your eyes off him." I pulled in one notch of flaps and eased the Cessna back to about 55 m.p.h.

We didn't have long to wait. About three miles down the road, the truck driver pulled into a church yard and cut his lights. The car continued toward Carnesville. Just as we began to speculate on what was going to happen next, the truck lights came back on.

"He's moving," Frank and Wally said in unison.

The truck turned around in the church yard and headed back in the direction from which it came. In a

short distance, it turned into the driveway of a farmhouse with three large chicken houses at the rear. The
headlights went out again but by the light of the Moon
we watched it continue on through the back yard and
down a hill. It backed up to one of the chicken houses.

"That's it. I'll keep going in a straight line so if they
do notice us, they won't suspect anything. I've got the
location pretty much pinned down. How about you,
Frank?"

"Yeah. That's Hickory Grove Church where he
turned around. I can find it."

When we got back to the airport after midnight, we
felt confident we had located a big distillery. ATF
Agent Bob Scott met us at the airport and Hay and I
left, flying back to Gunn Airfield. The investigation
was in good hands with Lane, Scott and the other
agents stationed in Athens and Gainesville.

I got home about 1:30 A.M., dead tired, but I was
back in the air the next morning with Wally Hay. We
found Frank Lane and Don Jones at the Athens
Airport.

"We've got good news. Jack Berry and Will Blocker
checked the chicken house before daylight this morning and found a huge upright steam boiler outfit,"
Frank reported.

We were all excited and began making plans to
observe both the stash house and the chicken house.
Area Supervisor Scott was calling in agents from
Cornelia and Gainesville to assist. Jack Berry, Guy
Wilson, Bill Ivey, Will Blocker, Bobby Cutshaw, Don
Jones, Frank Lane, Bill Maine, Bobby Wittemore,
James Stratigos and Harold Clemmons would all be

involved in round-the-clock observation of the two locations from December 2 through 7. Their surveillance produced a great deal of evidence which soon paid off.

Wally and I continued to fly and trail suspected vehicles, and on several occasions we went into the area on foot. On December 6 I joined Bill Ivey and Guy Wilson, who were observing the stash house. By seven that evening it was very dark. We had been watching and listening for about two hours when we heard a big diesel tractor-trailer coming toward us.

I was lying in a wooded area in high grass and weeds about three feet from the driveway. The huge tractor-trailer appeared out of the darkness like a giant mechanical monster bearing down on me. As it lumbered by, I had visions of driving it out myself, thinking it would make a great seizure and hurt the moonshiners' pocketbooks.

After the truck passed, I crawled through the high grass and brush to the edge of the farmyard. Five men were unloading cases of half-gallon fruit jars. There were at least a thousand cases of jars on that truck— enough for 6,000 gallons of moonshine. I watched them load two pickup trucks and put the remainder of the jars in the farmhouse. I recognized three of the men—John David, Sam Tate and Bobby Howard.

I quietly moved back to our meeting spot and called Bob Scott. "Listen, there are five men unloading jars from a tractor-trailer onto two pickup trucks. Let's hit the stash now. That way we can seize the tractor-trailer and two other trucks and arrest five men."

"We'd better wait and get a federal search warrant to be on firm ground," he cautioned.

"Ten-four," was my disappointed answer.

About two hours later the tractor-trailer eased out of the woods. Soon it was long gone. Around midnight, after all the activity died down, we slipped out of the area.

The next day Ivey and Wilson obtained a federal search warrant for the stash house and Frank Lane obtained one for the chicken house several miles away. That night just before dark, Ivey, Clemmons, Wilson, Maine and I dropped out and walked back into the area of the stash house. About 10:30 P.M. one of the trucks we had seen at the stash house and the still, drove in without lights.

This time Guy Wilson had a search warrant in his pocket and we figured it was time for action. Ivey radioed the agents at the still site. "We're going to hit the stash in 30 minutes."

"Ten-four. We'll hit the chicken house at the same time," came the reply.

Wilson and Maine silently moved out in the darkness to cover the south side of the building, while Clemmons and I eased in from the north end. As I crawled through the brush, three men were loading cases of half-gallon jars from the house onto the truck. They worked quietly, using very little light. Wilson was to make the initial move. I crouched against the front fender of the truck, hoping the moonshiners wouldn't see me before the others got into position.

"Federal officer with a search warrant," Wilson shouted. Bobby Howard was at the back of the truck bed and began to climb into the window of the cab head first. I jerked open the door and left him suspended halfway on the seat with his feet still on the window.

"You're under arrest!" I said, shoving his feet out of the window. He fell to the ground.

Meanwhile, Wilson and Clemmons arrested John David and Sam Tate inside the house.

Although we didn't get the tractor-trailer, we did seize three trucks, 800 cases of jars, 2,400 pounds of barley malt and all types of distilling equipment and fuel.

"670 to 739," I radioed to Blocker, "we've just hit our place. Is everything secure there?"

"Ten-four. We caught two and you know them both," he answered.

Leaving the prisoners with the other agents, I took the pickup truck and drove to the distillery site. I've been in the North Atlantic in winter storms, jumped out of airplanes, driven cars at high speed through city traffic chasing liquor cars and done a lot of other things, but raiding a still is without exception the most exciting, fun thing I have ever done. Catching them there at the stash house was fun but I'd rather have been at the still.

Blocker met me at the door. "We caught Skeeter Fields and Roy Lee in the still house. No one got away. It's a big one—15,000 gallons of mash and over 400 gallons of liquor."

The size of the distillery, the new equipment and the fact that Skeeter was the distiller all pointed to another J.R. operation. But as usual, J.R. was nowhere near the scene of the violation.

Talking with Scott and Lane after the seizure, we all agreed that working a big outfit like this for seven days in this particular area without it being "blown" was a good job. Sometimes things didn't work out this well, as we had found out a few months before in Habersham county.

Wally and I had little time to revel in the glory of the big seizure. We left the area at three in the morning and arrived back in Atlanta at five o'clock. There was just time enough to eat breakfast, shave and shower, before getting back in the air to trail another raw materials truck in the northwest section of the city with Jim West.

There were always plenty of law violators to pursue.

9.

AREA SUPERVISOR

THE FIRST THREE months of 1966 were hectic. Jim Daniels was not only finding large distilleries in north Georgia but he was also beginning to learn from John Guy and me about the abundance of moonshine being made in west Georgia around the Alabama line. Almost every day Jim or John would call with a new location to check. Adding this to my own flying surveillance missions and trying to keep up with all the paperwork left me very little time for my family or anything else.

In the 18 months from February 1964 through August 1965, Daniels located 82 illicit distilleries with 200,000 gallons of mash, more than 6,000 gallons of moonshine and property worth in excess of $67,000. 106 moonshiners were arrested as a result of his information.

In 1965, ATF had restructured to some extent, as government agencies tend to do periodically. A new position was created called Area Supervisor. It was a supervisory position that fell between the Resident Agent in Charge of a post of duty and the Assistant

Special Agent in Charge of a state. The highest position in the individual states was the Special Agent in Charge, who answered to the Chief of Criminal Enforcement for the region. There were seven states in the Southeast Region: North Carolina, South Carolina, Georgia, Florida, Alabama, Mississippi and Tennessee.

The new position of Area Supervisor was said to be preparation for being promoted to Assistant Special Agent in Charge and on up. The Area Supervisor usually was responsible two or more posts of duty, depending on the number of agents at each post. He was given a free hand to work with agents when he pleased, and except for having to make written evaluations of the agents and RAC's once a year, it was a great job.

One morning in May, Marvin Shaw, chief of the Special Investigative Section, came into our squad room. There were a couple of other agents preparing reports and shooting the breeze as Marvin walked in. The ones who weren't busy, got busy.

Shaw spoke to everyone, then walked over to my desk. "Let's go get a cup of coffee."

I thought, Oh, crap—what have I done wrong now? I had bent the rules occasionally, so I was a little apprehensive.

"Charley, how would you like to be Area Supervisor here in Atlanta?" Shaw got right to the point.

I was speechless for a moment, my mind racing. I was as happy as a pig in the sunshine where I was. Flying surveillance missions and raiding stills was my happy hunting ground and I didn't want to give that up, especially since I was the first agent to be given the green light to fly for ATF. Shaw could tell by my hesitation that I wasn't sure what to say.

"Of course you'll be working out of the Atlanta office with Atlanta and Newnan as your posts of duty. Charley, if you ever go any higher into supervision, you'll have to make it as Area Supervisor." As an afterthought, he added, "You can still fly."

Hmmm—maybe that wouldn't be too bad after all. I suspected that Bill Griffin was behind this offer, so I said, "Yes, sir, I'd like to try it, if Mr. Lane wants me."

"Good. We'll get that coffee some other time." Shaw left me at the elevator and walked back toward his office.

Thus began another phase in my career. The next week, Bob Lane interviewed me and I was on my way.

Although I hated to leave good friends and some of the best supervisors I ever had in Roy Longenecker, Ray Hahn, John Corbin, Bill Griffin and others in the regional office, I was excited to be taking on a new challenge.

The middle of June, 1966, I reported to Special Agent in Charge Bob Lane at the Georgia Branch Office in the Buckhead area of north Atlanta. M.L. Goodwin was the outgoing Area Supervisor, and he filled me in on everything he could about the job. I was also assigned his government vehicle, a 1964 Pontiac convertible. I could live with that. Lane showed me around and I immediately felt at home, having already worked with most of the people in the office.

Lane didn't mention anything about my flying activities, so I didn't either. I learned early on that sometimes a supervisor doesn't want to know everything.

Two days later Bob Lane called downstairs to my office. "Charley, Marvin Shaw just called. They need you to get an airplane and an observer and try to pick up a truckload of liquor coming out of Mississippi."

"I'm on the way!" That should break the ice. I could continue to fly while handling Area Supervisor duties.

On the way out of the office I asked Carolyn Welch, the post of duty clerk, secretary and jack-of-all-trades, "Try to get in touch with the Newnan office and tell them I'm on the way."

"Yes, sir, Mr. Weems."

At Gunn Airfield I picked up a Cessna 172 and was soon airborne.

"670 to any Newnan unit," I called, climbing to 5,000 feet.

"Go ahead, 670," Agent Tommy Stokes replied.

"Can you meet me at the Newnan dry dock in 20 minutes?"

"Ten-four, we'll be there."

I recognized the voice of Jim Whitehurst, the Resident Agent in Charge of the Newnan Post of Duty, who was listening in.

I landed at the Newnan airport and was met by Whitehurst, Stokes and Jimmy Satterfield. Jimmy had heard the radio traffic and was anxious to get in on whatever I was up to.

"We'll probably be following this truck for some time. I don't know where we'll end up. Satterfield, you go with me as observer. Stokes and Whitehurst can cover the vehicle on the ground until relieved."

While Jimmy stowed his gear in the airplane, I topped off with fuel.

We took off and headed west toward Highway 78, the main east-west road between Atlanta and Birmingham.

"He's just crossing the state line," the Alabama agents replied to Jimmy's call. "It's a big ten wheel black Ford with an aluminum body."

"Is it just passing a truck stop on the right?" asked Jimmy. Sometimes the ground units forgot that the state line wasn't painted on the landscape.

"Ten-four."

"We've got him!" Jimmy exclaimed. I swung the 172 back parallel to the highway.

The last time Satterfield and I had picked up a liquor truck in this area, a contract pilot was flying and he had accidentally put the 172 into a spin. Jimmy jokingly reminded me, "Just don't put us in a spin."

I didn't.

We followed the truck toward Atlanta and the Alabama agents dropped out and headed home. It was our baby now.

The truck took an unusual route, turning southeast through Carroll and Coweta counties. Stokes and Whitehurst were in contact with us from the ground and when the truck turned back north through Fayette and into Clayton County, we figured he must be getting pretty close to home.

"607 to 670," came Carl Koppe's familiar voice. "I'm just south of the Farmer's Market on old 41."

"Ten-four. Stand by, 607."

By this time it was beginning to get dark, and I had established contact with Atlanta Radar when we started north out of Newnan.

"97 Uniform—what is your altitude and what are your intentions?" The controller's voice was calm but insistent.

"We're at 2,000 feet but we can adjust either way. Looks like we'll be coming right through your traffic area," I replied.

"Roger, descend and maintain 1,800 feet. That will keep you under the incoming traffic."

I could see the landing lights of six or seven airliners lined up far into the distance on the approach to Atlanta International, and we were headed right into their path.

"Looks like he's pulling off at the Farmer's Market," Jimmy reported to the ground units. "Hold back."

I rolled the 172 into a steep bank and watched as the truck pulled to the rear of a big parking lot at a truck stop adjacent to the huge Georgia Farmers Market, just south of the Atlanta airport.

"607 to 670, I've got him in sight. We'll take it from here if you think he'll be here for a while."

Our fuel was down to about a quarter tank. "We'll go into the airport here if we can get a clearance and wait for word from the ground units," I told Jimmy, who relayed the message to the others.

"Atlanta Approach—this is Cessna 4597 Uniform. We need to land Atlanta if you can work us in." There was a long pause.

"Roger, 97 Uniform, understand you'll be landing Atlanta. We can accommodate you on Runway Two Zero if you can land in 1,500 feet and hold short of Two Seven Right."

"Roger, sounds good," I replied.

"Maintain 1,800 feet. Contact Atlanta Tower on 119.6."

Within ten minutes we were on the ground and getting fuel at one of the world's busiest airports.

Shortly after midnight Koppe called. "The driver has apparently settled in for the night. We've got enough people to cover the truck if you want to get some rest."

They got no argument from either Satterfield or me. I got home at three in the morning and slept a couple of hours. At 6:00 A.M. I went back to the Farmer's Market and met Koppe and Satterfield. The truck left the truck stop about noontime and we trailed it by car into DeKalb County. It pulled into another truck stop on Moreland Avenue and the driver disappeared. Koppe and I figured we had been seen by the violator. I called Ralph Elam, Chief of the DeKalb County Vice Squad, and John Crunkleton, DeKalb County detective, two of the finest law enforcement officers I ever had the pleasure to work with, and we seized the truck and 1,224 gallons of moonshine. We were disappointed about not coming up with an arrest, but we would get him the next time.

Large pan-type distillery, Fayette County, Georgia.

10.

THE APPARITION

THE JOB OF Area Supervisor entailed a multitude of duties but it gave me a distinct advantage over being a Regional Special Agent. There were at least 20 special agents I could call upon for help and they would always let me know when there was a big still to raid. It was the best of both worlds. SAC Bob Lane gave me a free hand and was totally supportive. Having previously been involved in aerial surveillance work all over the southeast, I was known by most of the agents. I continued to receive calls for aerial surveillance work from Georgia and adjacent states.

When I left the regional office, Wally Hay, who had become a close working partner with John Guy, Jim Daniels and me, was promoted to Group Supervisor over Regional Specials in North Carolina. Wally took over some of the paperwork involved in the air operation while John Guy retained overall responsibility for Daniels and the project. Wally worked long hours researching air operations in other federal agencies and proved that it was legal and proper for ATF agents to fly as pilots of leased aircraft. He wrote voluminous reports, justifications, and cost estimates and provided statistics to Personnel and Headquarters to justify the southeast region's operation of its own air force. Wally's work and the excellent results accomplished by Special Agent/Pilots in the southeast eventually led to ATF aircraft and pilots being located in all sections of the United States.

It wasn't easy. Any change in operational procedure had to be cleared by at least 47 lawyers in Headquarters who didn't have enough to keep them busy. They wrote extensive letters and opinions telling us why we _couldn't_ do something instead of trying to help get the job done.

The southeast region was very fortunate to have Bill Crewe as Regional Counsel. Bill was like most ATF agents. He would ofttimes give the answer to a legal dilemma by saying, "Seize the son of a bitch. We'll let the court decide if we had probable cause." That's the kind of answer I liked.

On two occasions I acted as defense attorney for Atlanta agents Frank Frazier and Chuck Lowe. Both times irate mothers swore out state warrants for the agents in Fayette County, Georgia.

On the first occasion, Sheriff Hugh Stinchcomb notified me that Harriet Thomas had taken out a warrant for Frazier. Some six months after that case was dismissed, I received a call from the sheriff that a Mrs. Allison had gone before the Justice of the Peace and taken out a warrant for Chuck Lowe, charging that he "jumped on her 14-year-old son."

It seems that Chuck and Harold Clemmons had raided the Allison home after a buy of moonshine and that Chuck had to restrain the young man by pushing him onto the couch. The J.P. knew that it was a frivolous warrant when he issued it, but the distraught mother insisted. The hearing was short and sweet, and as we were leaving the courthouse, I heard Stinchcomb tell Mrs. Allison that her complaint and misuse of the law to harass federal officers guaranteed her husband 18 months when he came to trial.

We had no more harassment charges coming out of Fayette County. It's too bad we don't have more sheriffs like Hugh Stinchcomb.

1966 was one of the busiest years of my life. I was flying missions two or three times a week, raiding distilleries an average of once a week and coordinating the activities of 22 special agents at the Atlanta and Newnan posts of duty. I was also responsible for the training and qualification of all the agents in the use of firearms and explosives.

But I was lucky. Some of the best agents in the country were stationed in Atlanta and Newnan. The Atlanta agents included Jim Elder, Carl Koppe, John Guy, Frank Frazier, Dale Harbolt, Charlie Hugueley, Chuck Lowe, Phil Orsini, Joe Powell, Byron Reed, Charles Stanfill, Jim Arey and Bob Todd. They worked the city of Atlanta and all the counties surrounding it.

Newnan is a small town about 40 miles south of Atlanta. Jim Whitehurst, John Rowden, David Greer, Pete Murphy, Tommy Stokes, Bill Barbary, John Kreeger, Emory Sheppard, J.P. Lott and Bill Hobbs worked a prolific distilling area from the Alabama line to the center of Georgia.

One Sunday afternoon in early August, I was enjoying a little game of ball with my sons, Joe and Charles. Dot came out on the front porch and although she tried to hide it, I could tell by her voice she was disappointed.

"There's a call for you from the Clayton County Police Department," she said. She knew I wouldn't have any more time for my family that Sunday.

At 5:30 P.M. I pulled into an area off Joy Lake Road, not far from where Jimmy Satterfield had been assaulted and had to shoot a moonshiner some years before.

Clayton County Police Captain James Parker was waiting for me. I had known James since my school days at Jonesboro High. His sister Jeanette was a classmate of mine, and after James became a Clayton County policeman we worked together every chance we got.

"We've got a report on a big still, but it might be 'hot'—the person who reported it was seen by the still hands," James filled me in. "Frank Frazier and Harold Clemmons are checking it now."

"578 to Parker—this thing is hot," the radio crackled. "There's no one here and they took the condenser with them." The radiator condenser was usually the most expensive portable item the violators could salvage when they left in a hurry.

"Okay, we'll come on in," James responded.

The distillery was a big one for that particular area. There were two 1,200-gallon fermenter stills and more than 220 gallons of moonshine ready to be moved out.

We finished up the destruction of the stills and liquor at nine that night and Frazier asked me to go with him to meet an informer in Fayette County. When I got home at 11:30 that night, all the family was sound asleep.

* * *

The next Sunday afternoon my home telephone rang. Dot answered it, then handed the receiver to me with that "here we go again" look in her eye.

"Every Sunday," she murmured.

"Charley, this is Peter Ghent in Anniston, Alabama. Roy Longenecker said you might be able to help me out." Peter was a real character, one of many who worked as special agents for ATF.

"I will if I can," I answered.

"We've got a big liquor stash located in Cleburne County, not far from the Georgia line. We think they'll move some liquor tonight, maybe into Georgia." That was his hook to get me interested. "John Petre and Bill Hobbs will be in the area for ground cover," he continued.

"What time and where?" I asked.

"How about the Carrollton airport at midnight?"

"I'll be there."

"When will you be back?" Dot wanted to know.

"I don't know—just look for me when you see me." She had heard that many times before.

I called Gunn Airfield and checked the weather with the FAA. "Severe clear" was the briefer's answer.

At least I wouldn't have to worry about thunderstorms tonight.

When I got to the airstrip that night around eleven, the 172 was waiting on the ramp. The weather was beautiful—a warm, clear Georgia night. I was the only one around and I reflected on how good the Lord had been to me. All my life I had wanted to be a pilot. Not only had I attained that dream, but I could fly at the government's expense. I tended to forget the many dangerous situations in which I had found myself.

It was midnight when I reached Carrollton. There's nothing quieter than a small local airport after midnight. Checking the windsock for the direction of the light wind, I turned final and lined up with the runway lights. I had received most of my flight training on a short airstrip in a wooded area, so I developed a habit of touching down very close to the end. This I did, and my landing lights pierced the darkness, revealing a strange apparition. Something was bobbing up and down, coming at me in the middle of the runway. I stopped the plane. As the thing got closer I could tell it was a man, but what was he doing? I pulled the fuel mixture and killed the engine. I didn't want the prop hitting this apparition, whatever it was.

The right door of the Cessna flew open.

"Are you Charley Weems?"

"Yeah. You must be Peter Ghent," I managed to say.

With that Peter began throwing his binoculars and crutches into the back of the plane. As he climbed into the front seat next to me I could see a big cast covering one foot and extending halfway up his leg.

"What happened to you?" I asked.

"I'll tell you later. We need to get going!"

I restarted the engine and soon we were over the Georgia-Alabama line.

"No activity," came the reply when Ghent contacted Petre. We climbed up to 9,500 feet and I throttled back and began slow flying, being careful not to stay over the same area too long.

As the hours wore on I thought about asking Peter again about his foot, but I decided against it. He obviously didn't want to talk about it. I found out later that he and some of the agents at the Anniston post of duty had located a used gyrocopter, a one-man flying contraption with a rotor on top and a small chain saw type engine in the rear which turns a propeller, pushing the vehicle forward. The forward motion through the air starts the top rotor spinning which provides the lift needed to fly the craft.

The Anniston POD was going to have its own air force in the person of Peter Ghent. The only problem was the engine wouldn't run. After the agents tinkered with it unsuccessfully for a week or so in their spare time, Peter became impatient to get it flying.

"Let's tie a rope to the front of the gyrocopter and pull it with a pickup truck," Peter suggested. "That way I can lift off the ground and at least get a feel for it. I've never flown one of these things before. We can repair the engine later."

All was prepared. A long tow rope was tied to the flying machine, with the other end attached to a fast pickup truck. One of the agents was assigned to drive the truck. Peter would fly, and the others were to be innocent bystanders.

"Let her go!" yelled Peter. The driver accelerated hard. Gravel and dust flew in all directions and the line suddenly tightened. The force of the jerk on the rope threw Ghent backward, causing him to pull back on the control stick. In a matter of seconds the gyrocopter, with Ghent struggling to maintain control, was wobbling 50 feet in the air. About that time, the rope broke, and the rest is history. Peter broke his leg and the Anniston post lost its gyrocopter—and its dream of an air force of its own.

The ATF radio brought me back to reality. "It doesn't look like we're going to have any activity tonight," John Petre reported.

"You mean this morning," I replied, looking at my watch. It was 4:00 A.M.

11.

HAIRY SITUATIONS

ONE OF THE first things that is taught and empha-
sized throughout a pilot's training is that an airplane
with four seats will not necessarily fly with four
people on board and full fuel tanks. Temperature,
altitude above sea level of the airport and weight of
the aircraft including fuel, passengers and luggage
all reduce the aircraft's ability to take off, especially
from short, rough airstrips.

The first week in September, the temperature was
in the 80's when I called Dodgie Stockmire at his
small airstrip near Villa Rica, Georgia. "I need a 172
for about an hour."

"We'll have one ready when you get here," he
replied. Dodgie had flown contract for ATF before and
knew our agents and some of our methods. This would
be my first flight out of his airstrip.

When I arrived John Kreeger, John Rowden and
Bill Hobbs were waiting for me. I began to have
second thoughts about getting out of this rough airstrip with four people in a 172—especially when three
of them weighed over 200 pounds. Kreeger, Rowden

and Hobbs were all former college football players. Even though I weighed only 160, we would still be well over the average of 170 pounds per passenger recommended by the 172's operating manual—and the runway was far shorter than the distance required for takeoff with this kind of load.

"I can carry two of you, but someone is going to have to stay on the ground," I advised.

Everyone wanted to fly. After a long discussion it was decided that Hobbs, the junior man at the post, would have to stay. Kreeger, Rowden and I loaded up. Hobbs was obviously disappointed. Trying to make everyone happy, as usual, I made a decision that almost cost us all our lives.

"Okay, come on," I called to Hobbs, who was walking slowly, head down, away from the plane. "We'll try it downhill."

One of the last sentences many pilots have uttered is "I think we can make it."

Hobbs eagerly piled into the rear seat with Rowden. The plane's tail dropped under the added weight. I knew then and there I had let my feelings override my good judgment, but it was too late now.

I fired up the 172 and taxied over the rough runway to the end. How I could think the four-cylinder, 145-horsepower engine, which wasn't in top-notch condition, was going to get this overloaded flying machine into the hot summer air in that short distance, I'll never know. It was an accident waiting to happen.

Reaching the end of the runway, I turned so that the tail extended over the end. I wanted every inch I could get, to gain the speed I would need to clear the trees at the other end of the runway.

I checked the engine and moved Kreeger's knees out of the way of the controls.

Trying to sound confident, I asked, "Is everybody ready?"

"All set," came their cheery reply.

With that, I shoved the throttle completely to the firewall and locked it while holding the brakes. The engine strained. I released the brakes and the 172 slowly began to roll. "Bump-bump" we hit an outcropping of granite in the runway and continued on. As we passed the hangar I glanced at the airspeed indicator—Sheee-it! We were only doing 45 miles per hour, but it was too late to stop now.

The end of the runway fell off sharply with the terrain. About a quarter-mile off the end, just past a wooded area, was a big lake. I knew it was now or never, and pulled back on the control wheel. The tail dropped even more and the stall warning horn came on and stayed on. I was committed with no more power, not much runway left and not enough airspeed. I pulled in a notch of flaps, hoping the added lift might help get the wheels off before we reached the edge of the runway—which by this time was imminent.

The stall warning horn sounded incessantly. I held the control wheel back in my lap while the Cessna struggled to get airborne. Just as we reached the end, within 50 feet of the treetops, the little plane lifted off.

The left wing dropped. I whipped the control wheel full right and let off some of the back pressure.

The 172 staggered out toward the trees. I gradually lessened the back pressure and cautiously glanced at the airspeed indicator. The plane was still on the verge of a complete stall but was beginning to gain a little speed. We swept through the treetops and finally reached the lake. I lowered the nose even more and although we lost a little precious altitude, we began to gain airspeed.

I began a gentle right turn to stay over the lake. Finally, after what seemed like hours, I began a slow climb. The stall warning horn had never stopped, and when I finally gained enough airspeed for it to cease, there was an audible sigh of relief.

No one had uttered one word all this time. The first one to speak was Hobbs.

"If you'll turn around and land, I'll get *out!*"

"The worst is over—no one gets out till we check this information and then we'll *all* get out," I said emphatically.

When we landed, Dodgie commented, "Kind of close, wasn't it?"

"A little," I replied, looking back at the end of the runway.

The good Lord was with me again. From that day till this, a period of 27 years and thousands of hours of flying time, I never overloaded an airplane again.

The efforts of the past few months were paying off. The big distilleries were coming now in bunches. One Saturday morning at five o'clock the telephone rang. It was always on my side of the bed so I answered it on the first ring.

"Charley, we've got information on a big outfit in DeKalb County. We need to get on it as soon as we can." Deputy Sheriff Ed Michaels didn't beat around the bush.

"What's the rush?" I asked sleepily.

"The husband and wife living on the still had a fight and the wife left, according to the informer. The still hands are afraid she'll report the still."

"All right. Where do you want to meet?" I asked, pulling on my pants.

"How about the IHOP on Moreland?"

"See you there, Mike."

As I pushed the government car through the early morning, I remembered my promise to take my boys fishing that day—but that would have to wait.

I met Michaels at the International House of Pancakes, then called Agent Jim Elder from a pay phone after I learned the details.

"I'll get Jimmy Satterfield to help us and we'll meet you at the IHOP as soon as possible," Jim said. He had recently been transferred to Atlanta, taking Satterfield's position as Resident Agent in Charge of the Atlanta Post of Duty. Jimmy had been promoted to Regional Special. Although I didn't know Elder prior to that, I liked him immediately and we became close friends, working together for many years.

As we drove down Flakes Mill Road in southwest DeKalb County, I began to wonder why anyone would set up a large outfit this close to civilization—but over the years I was to see several large distilleries set up in expensive residential areas and in very expensive homes. The moonshiners were coming up with new

techniques and most of the time they were successful—at least long enough for the backers to get a good
return on the money they invested.

We drove into an area of Flakes Mill that had
begun to grow within the last several years, with
residences replacing farm land. Mike had come up
with the information, and as we passed a driveway
leading back into some heavy woods, he spoke up.

"That's it—that's the drive to the still. There's a
house back there out of sight and a big chicken house
behind it. The still is supposed to be in the chicken
house."

"Well, it looks like a good place for one," Satterfield
commented. "When are we going to check it?"

"That's up to Charley and Jim," Mike answered.

"This will be a good one to cut your teeth on in
Atlanta," I told Elder, knowing he had a lot of experience raiding stills, but maybe none the size of this one.

"I'll get in touch with a couple of the Atlanta
agents. We'll check it this afternoon and call you at
home when we know something." Elder knew what he
was doing.

The fishing trip was definitely off, but I did get
home in time for a late lunch. I made a telephone call
to John Crunkleton.

"You and Elam want to help us on a big outfit
tonight?"

"Ralph's tied up but I can meet you at the Huddle
House at ten o'clock," was John's quick reply. Working as vice detectives in DeKalb, a bedroom county of
Atlanta, Crunkleton and Elam were always busy but
never failed to join us at any opportunity.

About one o'clock Sunday morning, Michaels came on the radio. "It's in there. We'll stay with it for a while."

By Monday morning, everyone involved had decided that the distillery was "hot." Elder called me at the office.

"How about getting Frank Kendall and Richard Ruth and meeting us out here on Flakes Mill. There's no one at the still site and we're going in at nine-thirty. Maybe Kendall and Ruth can lift some fingerprints." Ruth and Kendall were agents who specialized in fingerprint work and technical aids.

"Right. I'll be there shortly."

As we turned in the driveway I could see why the still was hot. There must have been a dozen officers, federal, state, county and city, at the site. Sometimes letting everyone in on the action can get out of hand.

The still was a big one. Even though we didn't arrest anyone, we did manage to hurt the man behind it financially. As we dynamited and cut up the big upright boiler and two 2,000-gallon steel stills, and poured out more than 10,000 gallons of mash and 850 gallons of moonshine, I was in my glory.

Three suspects were later identified from the fingerprints found, but without any other evidence we decided to chalk this one up to experience.

★ ★ ★

The next week, I was on the ground again with Whitehurst, Barbary, Lott and Greer about four miles north of Whitesburg, Georgia. Jim Daniels had located an outfit belonging to Fred Alta in an old farmhouse by trailing vehicles with the plane. When we made the seizure, we arrested Alta at the still with his still hand, Cris Levoice. It was another good catch. The Alta brothers had been in moonshining in a big way for years in west Georgia. With the 375 gallons of moonshine we poured out, the amount of liquor destroyed over the past several weeks was unbelievable.

The UFO

One night in late October, Jim Elder and I were in a 172 helping Atlanta and Gainesville agents trail a load of sugar out of Atlanta towards Cornelia. We worked for several hours trailing the truck and finally put him "in a hole." As we headed back to Atlanta in the clear cold night, we could see for miles. Jim left his observer's seat and joined me up front. We began to relax from the stress of the trail job.

All aircraft are required to have navigation lights, red on the left wing tip and green on the right, with a white taillight.

A small white light suddenly appeared in front of our plane, as if from nowhere.

"Do you see that light?" I asked Jim.

"Yeah! Where did it come from?"

The light was growing bigger and bigger by the second. The Cessna 172 has a top speed of about 135 and I knew we couldn't be overtaking another airplane that fast. In a matter of 15 or 20 seconds the light had grown big enough to fill the entire windscreen. I rolled right and down violently.

"Shee-it."

Turning back, we could see no sign of the light or anything else in the vicinity.

"Atlanta radar, this is 5347 Uniform. Do you have any other aircraft in our area?" I had contacted Atlanta Approach Control when we passed Gainesville on our way back into Atlanta.

"Negative, 47 Uniform, nothing in your area."

This was a time when there had been numerous reports of UFO's, several of which had proven to be hoaxes. I decided to let this one go.

"I won't say anything about this if you won't," I told Jim.

"Not me," he replied. "Someone would probably accuse us of being drunk on the job."

To this day I don't know what really happened that night—but I do know what I saw.

☆ ☆ ☆

Long surveillances of moonshine vehicles were becoming an almost everyday occurrence. It seemed that every week I would get a call from one of the surrounding states wanting the airplane to help trail someone. Word was getting around about our success. This time it was South Carolina.

I had just finished mowing the front yard one Saturday morning when Dot came out of the house.

"Jim Elder's on the phone," she called. And under her breath, "Another weekend."

"Charley, this is Jim Elder. I just got a call from agents I worked with in South Carolina. They're trailing a truck that belongs to one of their major violators. They say it was loaded with sugar and other raw materials in Baltimore, Maryland and looks like it's headed to a big still in Georgia."

"Okay. Call them back and tell them we'll be on the radio and in the air in 45 minutes. I'll get a plane from Peachtree-DeKalb airport and see if Wally Hay wants to go."

When the phone rang at Wally's home, he answered.

"Let's go fly," was all I said.

"I'm ready!"

"PDK in 30 minutes," and our conversation was over.

I had become friends with Wally, his wife Jean and their two sons, Andrew and Larry. On my first visit to their home, we sat and talked at the kitchen table. The boys came in and asked their mother if they could go out and play in the park. Having two sons of my own, I thought, They're too young to be going off somewhere alone to a public park.

"Sure," Jean said, "but put on your coats."

I was surprised. I didn't want to seem critical or nosey, but in a few minutes I couldn't help myself.

"Aren't they a little young to be going off to a park alone?" I asked.

Wally laughed. "They've been living in an apartment in New York City since they were babies. The only place they saw trees and grass was in a public park. When we moved into this house with its nice big back yard they naturally called the back yard a park."

So much for city living.

Wally was waiting for me when I got to PDK. He had already pre-flighted the airplane and was ready to go.

We headed northeast. Just outside Anderson, South Carolina, we spotted the truck and trailed it into the Athens, Georgia area. While the ground units kept the truck in sight, we made a pit stop, then picked up the truck again as it left Athens continuing southwest. By the time it passed through Macon we were all dead tired. Finally at Unadilla, Georgia the truck pulled into a wooded area behind a rural grocery store and parked. We notified the local agents and headed back to Atlanta.

It was four o'clock Sunday morning when I got home. Another 20 hour day.

ATF Agent Frank Frazier ready to chop up large distillery, Lumpkin County, Georgia.

Skeeter Fields and ATF Agent Bud Hazelip at large illicit distillery, Lumpkin County, Georgia.

Two "racehorses," Bud Hazelip and Frank Frazier, at large upright boiler distillery, Lumpkin County, Georgia.

12.

SHOOTOUT

ATF WAS STILL operating on a limited budget, although we were in better shape equipment-wise than in the past. In the summer of 1966, Frank Frazier and Phil Orsini began working undercover in the Atlanta metro area, while Special Agent C.A. Bodenheimer was conducting an undercover operation using an informer in the city to make small buys of moonshine from retailers. The money to make these small buys was furnished by the legal liquor industry through an organization called the Anti-Moonshine League. Frank and Phil used Purchase of Evidence money furnished by ATF and made wholesale buys of liquor ranging from 20 to 200 gallons at a time.

By the end of September, Frazier and Orsini had bought moonshine from more than 20 people in the Atlanta metro area, while Bodenheimer's informer had bought from 150 retailers. Now it was time to "swoop down on 'em," as old-time agent Ed Carswell always said.

It was going to be a huge undertaking to arrest and round up all these people in a giant sweep of the area. Frank and Phil spent two days securing state and federal arrest warrants. I coordinated by bringing in agents from Newnan and other posts of duty to assist. City and county police officers from Fulton and DeKalb counties and a number of state revenue agents were also on hand.

All day Sunday, October 16 we worked getting ready for the roundup that night. By 8:30 P.M. our office just off Peachtree Road was a beehive of activity. We selected two-man teams, usually pairing an ATF agent with one state agent or one local officer so that at least one member of the team was familiar with the territory they would be working. Each team was given a handful of warrants to serve and to make arrests.

Each defendant would have to be fingerprinted and photographed and then placed in the Fulton County Jail to await a hearing.

I remained in the Atlanta office to relay messages and furnish assistance where it was needed. It was decided that Frazier and Orsini would initiate the operation by making the first arrest. Herman Sidney was selected since he dealt in large amounts of moonshine and had numerous connections in the liquor business. Orsini made a telephone call.

"He'll meet us on 41 Highway near Kennesaw Mountain."

"Harbolt, Koppe and I will be your cover," Jim Elder volunteered.

On an undercover knock-off, we never knew how things would end up. This was one of those cases. Frazier had years of experience in undercover work and making arrests but he felt apprehensive about this one. He didn't let anyone know, but did tell Orsini to carry an extra pistol. Frank always carried two.

The plan was set. As soon as Frazier and Orsini arrested Sidney, the others would start picking up the remainder of the nearly 200 bootleggers. By 9:00 P.M. all the teams had moved out, some having to travel as much as 40 miles to pick up their violators.

In previous dealings with Sidney, he had given the appearance of a middle-man operator who brought in large amounts of moonshine and resold it in case lots. He seemed the least likely of the 25 wholesalers to give us any trouble. How wrong we were!

In the early sixties ATF had begun to release public relations articles and call in newsmen on seizures in an effort to educate the public as to the magnitude of the moonshine problem in the southeast. Reporters for the Atlanta papers had been alerted and we even considered putting a reporter and an agent in the trunk of the undercover Chrysler to get a firsthand account of Sidney's arrest. Thank the Lord we didn't.

It was a dark night with no Moon. Frazier and Orsini waited at a roadside park near Kennesaw Mountain, the site of one of the bloodiest battles of the War Between the States. Frank continued to have reservations about the possible outcome of tonight's work. He and Orsini had been buying moonshine for the past several months and the moonshiners were beginning to get a little suspicious of them. They had recently been turned down by two wholesalers they had bought liquor from and it appeared that the word might be out.

"You think he'll show?" Orsini asked.

Frazier was deep in thought. Just as he was about to answer, a car pulled into the small roadside park. Frank blinked his headlights and the car pulled alongside.

Sidney appeared nervous. "Follow me," he said curtly.

Shrugging, Frank fired up the big Chrysler. Orsini slid a small radio from beneath the seat and contacted Jim Elder. "Stay with us."

"Ten-four."

Frazier glanced in the mirror as he crested a hill, just in time to see headlights come on behind him. He felt better. As their headlights illuminated the Marietta City Limits sign, both agents wondered what was next. They drove through a ghetto area with small shotgun houses and dimly lit alleys, finally stopping at a dead end blocked by junked cars.

"Damn, it's dark," commented Orsini.

Sidney suddenly appeared at their car. "Come on in."

As they followed him into the five-room house, they could hear sounds of people talking and playing cards in an adjoining room.

"I haven't got anything tonight," Sidney said, more comfortable now in his own environment.

"We need ten cases (60 gallons) tonight," Frank persisted.

"Well, all right. I'll call a man I know." With that, Sidney disappeared into the next room.

Orsini and Frazier looked at each other. They both knew it could be a trap.

A minute later, Sidney came back into the room looking a little more self-confident. "I couldn't find any. Everyone seemed to be out."

Knowing that 30 officers were waiting in Atlanta to begin their roundup and that Sidney was not going to sell any whiskey tonight, Frank nodded to Orsini. "Well, let's go. We'll have to check with Boxhead."

As they walked out into the inky blackness, Frank turned back to the door where Sidney stood. "Oh, I wanted to tell you something," Frazier mumbled under his breath.

Sidney, curious as to what Frazier said, ventured further out into the yard. "What did you say?"

"I said, we're federal officers. You're under arrest." Frank shined the flashlight on his gold shield.

"I'm not going," said Sidney, backing away.

Orsini grabbed one arm. Frazier, trying to hold his flashlight and a radio in one hand and Sidney with the other, shouted, "You're *going!* "

The agents began to push the bootlegger into the back seat of the Chrysler. He suddenly submitted, saying, "I don't want no trouble. I don't want no trouble."

Frazier, standing by the open right front door, helped Sidney into the rear of the car while Orsini began to handcuff the prisoner. When Frazier released Sidney to call Elder on the radio, Sidney suddenly jerked loose.

Hitting Orsini in the jaw with his elbow, he said, "Look here, man."

Frazier keyed the mike of the ATF radio and yelled, "Come on in."

BLAM—a shot rang out from the rear seat, the bullet barely missing the top of Orsini's ear.

"He's got a gun!" screamed Orsini, falling backwards out of the car.

BLAM—another shot rang out from the back seat, hitting Frazier in the upper left arm. Frazier, his arm burning intensely, stuck his five-shot snub nose .38 into the car and emptied it at point blank range toward the gun flashes. Throwing down the .38, Frank pulled his .357 magnum. Sidney came out of the back seat still shooting. Frazier fired three more shots. Meanwhile, Orsini had emptied his .38 and was trying to get his second gun into action. Frazier was hit again, this time in the center of the chest. The force knocked him down. He propped himself up against the Chrysler and continued to exchange fire with Sidney, who was trying to take cover under a junked car.

By the time Sidney ran out of ammunition and stopped firing, a total of 21 shots had been fired in far less time than it takes to tell about it.

There was a frantic call on the office radio base station.

"448 to 670, I'm headed up to the Kennestone Hospital in Marietta. Frank Frazier's been shot. Don't know his condition." It was Elder.

"I'm on the way. 670 clear," I replied.

Special Agent in Charge Bob Lane was working upstairs and I quickly told him where I was going.

"I'll meet you in the parking lot," he said without hesitation.

I liked that. I had the good fortune to work for some of the best supervisors in ATF and I appreciated their support.

When we arrived at the hospital, I went immediately to Emergency, identified myself as Frank's supervisor and was shown into one of the operating rooms. My good friend Frank looked bad. He had been hit twice, once in the upper left arm and once in the chest.

"How ya doing, Frank?"

He had been sedated but he looked up and said, "I'm glad to see you here—don't let them take my arm off!"

"Don't worry, Frank, nobody's going to take your arm off," I replied emphatically. "You just take it easy and we'll be right outside till they get through patching you up."

Frank managed a weak smile and drifted back into his twilight sleep. The doctor explained that although the bone was shattered in Frank's arm, they could save it and that fortunately, the wound in his chest was superficial.

On October 28, 12 days after the shootout, Herman Sidney was released from Kennestone Hospital. Jim Elder and I were waiting for him. I couldn't help but enjoy putting handcuffs on this guy. Having been shot five times, twice in the stomach, he was still walking slowly and I sort of enjoyed seeing him suffer. He had made Frazier suffer. After we fingerprinted and photographed Sidney, Phil Orsini had the pleasure of putting him in the Fulton County Jail pending a bond hearing.

Sidney had a three-page police record dating back to 1952. It showed a total of 34 arrests and included cutting one person, shooting at another, threatening with a gun, carrying a concealed weapon, resisting arrest, eluding officers and contempt of court, just to name a few. Sometimes looks can be deceiving.

Frazier, Orsini and Sidney were all lucky that no one was killed. After this episode Frank not only wore two guns—he added a third.

The Rookie

On the morning following the shooting of Frank Frazier and the roundup of 200 bootleggers in Atlanta, Jim Arey reported for duty at the Atlanta office. Jim was a good-looking young man, rosy cheeked and just out of college. He was from Salisbury, N.C. and looked as innocent as the driven snow.

As he pushed his way past foul-smelling bootleggers and some foul-smelling officers there was a bewildered look on his face. He must have wondered what he had gotten himself into. The place was a madhouse with stragglers still being brought in for processing and paperwork stacked on all the desks.

Finally, a big rough-looking guy came over to where Arey was standing. Jim later described him as looking like a man who had played linebacker for the Green Bay Packers for ten years and spent his spare time fighting for fun in redneck bars.

The agent explained that we were in the process of arresting a bunch of bootleggers and brought him into my office. Arey's first question to me was, "Does this go on *all* the time?"

"Almost," I said jokingly.

"Who's that guy that brought me in here?" was his next question.

"That's Joe Powell. He looks tough and is tough. He's a good agent."

Later Arey asked Joe why he was wearing a body cast and Joe told him he broke his back raiding a still, adding to Arey's apprehension.

After getting acquainted with Arey, I decided he might as well get the full treatment his first day. The big black Chrysler 300C Frazier had been driving the night before was parked in the lot at the rear of our office building.

"You should have been here last night," I told Arey as we walked across the parking lot. "This is the car two of our agents were in when they got into a shootout with a bootlegger."

Several bullet holes were plainly visible in the car's right front door and hood. Fresh blood had run down the door, both on the inside and outside. It looked almost as gory as the car Bonnie and Clyde were ambushed in. Arey took it all in with very few comments.

I'm sure he did a lot of soul-searching that night, alone in his rented room.

Three weeks later, Jim Elder caught me as I was walking into the office.

"Charley, Jim Arey's wife is coming into town on a bus this morning at eleven. We're going to play a little trick on him, if you'll go along."

"Sure."

"He's supposed to leave at ten o'clock to pick her up. About thirty minutes before that, I'm going to come in and announce that I need every agent here to go on a raid—now—and that I don't know how long we'll be gone. Everyone will start getting their gear together and when he says something about his wife, you volunteer to go pick her up."

"Sounds good," I agreed.

Everything went as planned. I acted surprised when Elder and the other agents began leaving. Then Jim brought Arey over to my office.

"Charley can pick up your wife," Jim told him.

Arey looked a little unsure about this arrangement. "She'll be on the eleven o'clock bus from Raleigh. She's got blue eyes and blond hair." He looked back at Elder and around the office to see if anyone could help him out of this dilemma. "She don't know anyone in Atlanta and certainly don't know you," he said, almost pleading.

By this time everyone was either feeling sorry for him or laughing so hard that we could keep our joke no longer.

"You assholes," Jim mumbled under his breath. He was right. We were—but we weren't through yet.

As soon as Arey left to go pick up his wife, there was a flurry of activity. I went over to the squad room to see what was going on.

"Look on Jim Arey's desk," Elder said.

On the desk was an 8 by 10 framed photograph of a beautiful young girl. On the front was written in very feminine handwriting, "To Jim, with all my love, Mickie."

"Is this Jim's wife?" I asked.

"Nope," several agents answered at once. "Someone found this picture and we got Angie McCurdy to sign it for us. You think his wife will like it?"

"She'll kill him. That's dirty."

Arey had told us he was going to bring his wife by the office so she could meet us. That was a mistake. Of course everyone was on hand in the squad room when Jim and his wife walked in. After we had all introduced ourselves she asked, "Where's your desk?"

Arey hadn't noticed the new picture on his desk until now, and his face turned brilliant red.

"It's that one there," Elder said with a sly grin.

When Arey's wife picked up the picture we could contain ourselves no longer. Everyone burst out laughing. Mrs. Arey realized then it was a joke but in the few seconds before we all laughed, she wasn't so sure.

When Jim survived that first month around that bunch of roughnecks and practical jokers, I knew he would make it in ATF. From that day till this, Arey has made an excellent agent.

Cadillac driven by Herman Sidney. Note bullet hole in fin.

Rear window of Chrysler 300C used by Agents Frazier and Orsini, showing bullet holes in window and side panel.

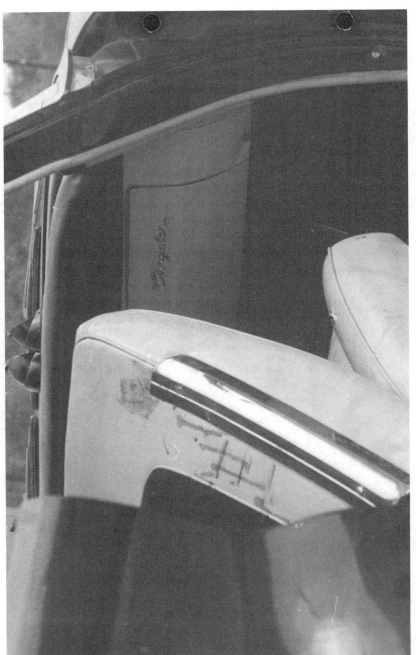

View of interior of Chrysler showing bloodstains and bullet holes.

13.
MONEY TALKS

THE TREASURY DEPARTMENT began to beef up ATF with new agents in the latter part of 1966. I was fortunate that men the caliber of Chuck Lowe, Dale Harbolt and Chuck Stanfill were assigned to the Atlanta office, while John Rowden was assigned to Newnan. Harbolt, Rowden and Stanfill had worked together as detectives for the Oklahoma City Police Department. They adjusted quickly to ATF's rather unique way of enforcing the law.

We had undercover agents working in most areas around Atlanta on an ongoing basis. Harold Clemmons and Jim Arey made numerous buys of moonshine in Fayette and Spalding counties and there were always raids to make and warrants to serve. My flying work continued, both in Georgia and Alabama. It was commonplace to have three or four active stills located at one time.

Our enforcement activities put tremendous pressure on the moonshiners and bootleggers, as well as on the federal and state officers. We worked day and night and could see no end to it, but we enjoyed every moment.

On a Saturday night in March of '67 the telephone rang. I had just gone to bed.

"Charley, this is Howard Smith. We've got something good. Could you meet me at the Clayton-Henry county line on 42 Highway?"

"I'll be there in 30 minutes," I said and began to dress.

Chief Howard Smith of the Clayton County Police had been someone I looked up to and admired since I was a youngster in grammar school. He was one of the first Clayton County patrolmen and had advanced to the position of chief. There was none better.

At 11:30 that night I pulled into an abandoned service station on Highway 42 where Howard and Detective Raby were waiting.

"We've got information that there's over a thousand gallons of liquor at a farmhouse down here on the line. It's so close that I don't know if the house is in Clayton or Henry County. I think it would be best if you put it in federal court. We need to hit it as soon as possible."

"Sounds good to me. 670 to any Atlanta unit," I called on the ATF frequency.

"Go ahead, 670."

I recognized Jim Elder's voice. "Jim, how about getting some agents together and meeting Chief Smith at the Clayton-Henry county line on U.S. Highway 42. Looks like we've got some work to do." That was the understatement of the night.

"Let's go," I said, firing up the Pontiac.

"Raby, you go with Charley and show him the house. I'll wait here for the other ATF men and lead them in," said Howard.

I had a good feeling about this one, but never expected to find what we did. Turning off 42, Raby and I hit a small country road that formed a "T" with another asphalt road in a wooded area that had once been farmland.

"That's it," Raby said as we passed an old farmhouse with several sheds, a big barn and a large van and horse trailer in the side yard.

"I can smell it," I said, "but we need to get more probable cause to raid without a warrant. We'll walk in."

In ten minutes we came upon more than 300 gallons of moonshine sitting at the edge of the yard in plain sight. A light was on in the rear of the house.

"Raby, you take the front door and I'll get the back. It looks like somebody's moving around in there. We'd better get what we can—now!"

Giving Raby time to get to the front door, I walked up on the back porch and knocked. The back porch light came on.

Maybe I should have waited for backup, I thought. Too late now. I knocked again. A woman in her early forties opened the door.

"I'm Charley Weems, a federal officer. Is anyone else in the house?"

"No, sir," she answered.

I knew she was telling the truth.

"What's your name?"

"Opal Doris."

"Mrs. Doris, you're under arrest for possession of nontaxpaid whiskey," I said. I advised her of her constitutional rights against self-incrimination and she said she preferred not to make a statement until she talked to her lawyer.

Thirty minutes later Elder, Harbolt, Stanfill, Frazier, Arey and Clemmons arrived with Chief Smith.

As it turned out the stash house was in Henry County. Mrs. Doris was taken to the Fulton County Jail to await a bond hearing, and we began to take inventory of what we had seized. Moonshine was stacked high in the barn and the adjoining shed. The van and horse trailer contained more than 800 gallons. Everywhere we looked there was a stack of moonshine—a total of 3,365 gallons. It was the most moonshine I had ever seen in one place. We also seized more than 4,000 pounds of sugar, the GMC van and the horse trailer for forfeiture.

The next morning we began the huge task of destroying the liquor. Our procedure was to destroy it where we found it. Only when we seized a car or truck in the city did we transport moonshine any distance before pouring it out. The environmentalists of today would scream to high heaven if they saw us pouring large quantities of alcohol on the ground or city streets, but we did it all the time. On that morning moonshine was flowing like a stream down the ditches away from the house and barn, and cut-up one gallon plastic jugs were stacked high all over the premises. I really enjoyed the work.

Later that same month Jim West was furnished information that led us to the origin of all this moonshine. On March 28, West called from the regional office. "Charley, I've got something to show you—but come alone."

Jim West was one of the best undercover agents in ATF. I worked with him on all types of cases and knew he was a tenacious and well qualified agent. He showed no fear of anyone or anything except flying near thunderstorms—but more on that later.

I picked West up at the regional office and drove south out of Atlanta. Jim began to fill me in on some of the details.

"An informer called me last night and said there's a big upright boiler still in a barn in Fayette County. Charley, this information has to be kept close. Don't tell anyone that I gave it to you. These people have inside connections with several state agents and we'll have to keep radio traffic to a minimum. You'll understand when I tell you later who it belongs to—if it's there. Go on into Fayetteville and take Highway 54 west."

"Okay," was my only comment. I knew Jim was telling me all I needed for now.

About six miles west of Fayetteville, Jim suddenly said, "Turn right at the next road."

I quickly made a mental note of our location and wheeled onto the small blacktop. We were in a well-kept, rural farming area.

I worked as a field agent for several years in Fayette and surrounding counties south of Atlanta, but never had reason to check this area before. We made a left on another blacktop road and approached a big farm pond on the left.

"It's the next house on the left." Jim said.

There was a long driveway leading to a nice brick house. A big barn stood off to the left, partially hidden behind a small hill.

"That's an awful nice place to have a still," I commented.

"J.R. puts them in nice places," West retorted.

West knew of my previous frustrations with J.R. Turner, whom I had pursued for three years from '62 through '64, and who had outsmarted me at every turn. Even though I finally found out the reasons, it still hurt my pride to know I wasn't able to get enough evidence to take him to trial.

"This is *great* , Jim!"

"I've got this informer on the inside. If you can make a known seizure and arrest someone at this distillery we should be able to tie J.R. in."

"Damn, I hope so." I was elated.

I dropped West off in downtown Atlanta, then contacted Jim Elder. We met at the branch office.

"You and I have something we need to check tonight, so don't make any other plans. We need someone not known in the Atlanta area to drop us out."

"Emory Sheppard and Roy Moore are in town for court. I'll get them lined up. How long will it take?"

"From about eleven tonight until daylight. That should give us plenty of time."

"We'll be ready."

"I'll be on the radio if you need me," I told Carolyn Welch as I left the office. Peachtree-DeKalb Airport was about a 20 minute drive from the office and within the hour I was in a Cessna 172 headed south. Flying straight and level at 3,500 feet, I passed over the west side of the suspect area in Fayette County. Looking at an area from above became an invaluable tool in determining the best and safest access route to go in on the ground. About five miles to the south I began a slow 180-degree turn and flew back over, this time on the east side. We could drop out on foot about a mile from the farm on another road and approach it across a large pasture from the rear.

That night it was very dark.

"After we drop out, get completely out of the area for three hours. We'll try to make radio contact about two o'clock. If you don't hear us, park behind the Sandy Creek Church. That should be close enough. Wait another half hour and then come back through where you dropped us out," I told Sheppard.

We always tried to make contingency plans in case a radio went dead. Sheppard and Moore agreed, then left.

By this time it was almost midnight and the Moon was trying to shed a little light as Elder and I made our way across the pasture.

"How much further?" Jim whispered.

Making your way across open fields and through woods at night becomes almost second nature after you've done it for years. We always moved without lights and developed an instinct for direction. Some were better at it than others but there was no substitute for experience—and looking at the area from the air.

Suddenly it hit me—the strong, pungent odor of mash. There was no wind that night and I knew we must be very close to the still. Elder smelled it, too. We both froze like bird dogs pointing quail. Peering intently, I caught the straight outline of a roof to our right and just below the crest of a hill. I eased my way slowly in that direction, Jim right on my heels. He nudged me.

"That's the barn. The house is off to the left," he whispered.

I looked left and could see a faint glow coming from a bathroom window.

"We've got probable cause to get a warrant but we need to make sure."

We edged closer to the barn. About 50 yards from the barn, the solid grassy pasture began to feel soft under my feet. I squatted down and felt the ground. There was straw covering a big area between us and the barn.

"This is the mash pit," I whispered.

Concealing large distilleries like this produced several problems for the moonshiners other than just hiding the stills and equipment. Several hundred gallons of spent mash would have to be dumped after each run. If allowed to remain above ground it would put out a strong odor and kill all the surrounding vegetation. The moonshiners, being true conservationists, would usually dig a huge mash pit, something like a drain field for a septic tank, then pump the mash into it. They would cover the pit with a ground-level roof of timber and then cover the entire area with earth, sometimes sowing grass to camouflage it. They really weren't interested so much in conservation as in their freedom. Any large area of dead vegetation seen from the air or on the ground served as a red flag to ATF agents.

Headlights flashed across the pasture. A big truck was turning into the driveway from the public road.

The lights went out immediately. Jim and I flattened ourselves on the ground. The truck continued up the driveway and flashed its lights once as it passed the house. It backed up to the barn. In the moonlight I could see the outlines of two men leaving the house. They began helping the driver unload 100-pound bags of sugar from the truck.

"That's it," I whispered. "Let's ease out of here."

Sheppard and Moore picked us up at 2:30 A.M. "We need to get on this as soon as we can," I told Jim. "Can you get some men on the ground by tonight?"

"You bet."

"Good—but be careful and keep everything as close to your vest as you can. We can call in the state and local officers later. The man behind this has a lot of connections. And keep the radio traffic to a minimum—we can't be too careful."

Elder nodded. He hadn't been in Atlanta long, but he knew we had had some problems with information being leaked.

Jim West was pleased but cautious when I told him we had located the distillery. "Charley, be careful with it. You know J.R. Don't try to stay with it too long or you won't catch anyone—that bunch has ways of finding things out. I've got someone who will tie it all together once you catch this outfit. Just be sure you get someone!"

"We'll do our best."

That night, Chuck Lowe and Chuck Stanfill were on the ground watching the house and barn. They continued surveillance for two days, alternating with Harold Clemmons and Jim Arey. About noontime on the 31st of March, Arey and I received a call from the still area.

"Two men just left in a big one and a half-ton Ford U-Haul truck. We've seen them both in the still house."

"Is the truck loaded?"

"We don't know."

"Jim, here we go!"

We were backed up into a grove of trees in order to see Tyrone Road and any vehicle that might pass. Jim Elder and Harold Clemmons were covering the other end of the road.

"There he goes!" Arey exclaimed.

As the truck topped the next hill, I eased the Pontiac convertible out onto the road. I knew Arey was anxious to arrest someone, so I hit passing gear and we soon had the truck in sight.

"We gonna stop him?"

"We'll just see where he's going for now," I answered.

The truck turned toward Atlanta on I-85. He took the Old National Highway exit and stopped at a telephone booth at a Texaco station.

"We'd better get them before they make that phone call. Jim, you take the passenger side. I'll get the driver. Keep your jacket over your gun and walk toward the telephone. If he gets out, get him. If not, go to the passenger side of the cab. I'll give you time, then I'll take the driver's side."

Everything worked as planned. I arrested Jerry Staywick and Arey arrested Ed Peck. Both had extensive arrest records for moonshining.

I called Elder. "We've got them at Old National Highway and I-85. You can come and get them."

In ten minutes Elder and Clemmons arrived. They took charge of the truck and the prisoners. "When these two don't return, the others might leave. We've got a federal warrant for the farm and can hit it any time," suggested Elder.

"Suits me. Is everyone in place around the location?"

"Yeah. We've got Frank Frazier, Chuck Stanfill, Hugh Merrill and Chuck Connor around the site. That should have them covered. We'll just drive in and see what happens!"

Agent Charlie Hugueley had gone to Fayetteville to pick up my old friend, Sheriff Hugh Stinchcomb. They were waiting at the other end of the public road that ran by the still house.

"Charlie, you can start in," I radioed. "We should get to the driveway about the same time."

As I rounded a curve in the road, Hugueley and Stinchcomb were approaching from the other direction. We both tried to get to the driveway first and I just barely nosed him out. Arey was enjoying every minute. We barreled up the driveway toward the house, dust boiling up from under the Pontiac.

Suddenly, a woman's head popped out of the basement door. We slid up to the side of the house and the woman bolted from the door, disappearing around back. Paul Stevens emerged from the basement and Charlie Hugueley caught him immediately. I plunged around the house and almost ran over a very frightened Ruby Peck. "You're under arrest," I told her, taking her arm. "We have a search warrant for the house."

"I need to go to the bathroom," was her only comment.

Sudden fright will do that.

In the basement we found 620 gallons of moonshine in a gigantic mixing tank, along with thousands of plastic jugs. In the barn was a huge illegal distillery. The 4,000-gallon steel tank still was hot. There were more than 15,000 gallons of fermenting mash. They were producing more than 600 gallons of moonshine every day of the week. It was a big operation, certainly one of J.R.'s.

Most large distilleries of this type used two automobile radiators hooked up in series to condense the alcohol steam into moonshine. This one had *three* large radiators in series. They could make a lot of moonshine in a short time.

Jim West was happy the next day when I briefed him on the seizure and arrests. "This should tie up your old nemesis, J.R., this time," he said confidently. But in the end, even West underestimated the power and influence of J.R.'s money.

A north Georgia woman had given West a complete and revealing statement as to J.R.'s ties to this distillery and others. However, just before the case came to trial, the woman suffered a sudden lapse of memory. And coincidentally, she suddenly acquired a new double-wide mobile home. They say everyone has a price.

J.R. had escaped justice once more.

14.

THE BLUFF

SEVERAL MONTHS PRIOR to my being assigned to the Atlanta Branch Office, Newnan agents had seized a like-new 1964 Dodge Dart with a 426 cubic-inch Hemi engine. During those years Chrysler was into producing muscle cars for stock car racers and made some of the high performance engines available to the general public. Plymouths and Dodges running this engine were burning up racetracks and drag strips all over the country. Looking at the outward appearance of the little Dart you would never think it had an engine that could blow away any production vehicle of that time, including the 427 Ford, in a drag race. It was unbeatable.

When the Dodge was forfeited by the federal court to the Treasury Department, I requested it for official use and Bob Lane assigned it to me. I had discovered that a six-volt siren would operate on a vehicle with a 12-volt system. Most cars prior to 1956 had a six-volt electrical system. With the change to 12-volt systems we had to find a way to use the sirens from the old days. These sirens would work but if held on for more than two or three seconds they would burn up, literally. The initial wail of the siren was instantaneous. It didn't wind up slowly, it screamed wide open immediately and would scare the pants off anyone who wasn't expecting it. I put one on the Dart.

One spring night Jim Elder and I had been flying on a surveillance mission out of Peachtree-DeKalb. Around one in the morning we were on our way back to our office near Lenox Square. The streets were deserted except for a few party-goers. We stopped at a red light. The windows were down and as we waited for the light to change, a brand new 1968 Buick Electra convertible pulled up alongside. The top was down and three obviously inebriated couples were feeling no pain. They were laughing and enjoying themselves in the warm spring night. I glanced over at the car. The young man on the passenger side remarked to me, "You wanna drag—GrandPAW?" I was 40 years old and resented being called a grandpa. Elder snickered.

"Your bulldog mouth might be overloading your poodle dog ass," I commented under my breath. The light changed. The driver of the Buick floorboarded it and to my surprise it did get away pretty well. When he was about half a car length ahead of me I kicked in the four-barrel carburetor on the Dodge and we flashed by him like he was standing still. I let off the accelerator and waited. Va-Roooom—the Buick came by wide open, with all on board laughing.

EEEEyouuuu—my siren screamed in the quiet night. The Buick seemed to stop in mid-air. All six heads began to swivel as though caught in a whirlwind. The Buick pulled over and Elder waved as we passed. We left them sitting at the curb, bewildered. It was a great night for grandpas.

☆ ☆ ☆

On Friday, April 21, my government radio crackled. "670, call your office as soon as possible." It was Carolyn Welch at the Atlanta office. I whipped into the next service station and made the call.

"Mr. Weems, Alabama agents are trailing a black 1962 Pontiac loaded with liquor. It's on Highway 78 between Anniston and Heflin, headed toward the Georgia line. They want us to pick it up. I think they're using an airplane."

"We'll get on it."

It was almost 5:30 P.M.

"670 to any unit."

"670, this is 607. Do you need any help?" Carl Koppe, a thorn in the side of liquor haulers in the Atlanta area for the last 15 years, was on the job as usual.

"Meet me at the KK on Ponce DeLeon. We'll probably need another car if anyone else is on the air," I said.

Pulling into the Krispy Kreme shop I saw Koppe, Bob Todd and Frank Frazier inside drinking coffee. Interstate 20 was under construction west of Atlanta and was open only as far as the intersection of Georgia Highway 5 near Douglasville. We knew the Pontiac would probably take U.S. 78 to Georgia 5 and then I-20 into Atlanta.

"Frank, if you'll set up about halfway between the end of I-20 and the Chattahoochee River, I'll go to Highway 5 and try to pick him up when he hits I-20.

Koppe, you and Todd can wait at the river and we should be able to contact each other by radio. I'll trail him to Frank's location and then Frazier and I will switch off and trail him on into town. When you get on him, we'll box him in and knock him off."

"Sounds good."

Grabbing a dozen donuts to go, we headed west. It was beginning to get dark. By the time I reached the end of I-20 at Georgia 5, I could hear radio traffic from the Alabama agents in the contract plane. I advised them of my location and they sounded relieved.

"We're about out of fuel, so we're pulling off. It's all yours. He's halfway between Villa Rica and Douglasville on Highway 78. Good luck."

Looking for a place to park without arousing suspicion and yet within sight of Highway 5, I spotted a new service station being built in anticipation of the traffic the finished interstate highway would generate. A blacktop driveway ran alongside the station and up a small hill to a yard where a house once stood. This was ideal. I could sit on this bluff overlooking the service station, see every vehicle that passed on Highway 5 and have quick access to the suspect when he hit I-20. Sitting in the shelter of the huge oak trees, I tried to make radio contact with Frazier and Koppe. No joy. Well, when he comes by I'll just pull in behind him and as we get closer to Atlanta I'll be able to contact someone, I thought. The best laid plans....

Being alone, I couldn't take my eyes off the highway. A black '62 Pontiac suddenly appeared in front of the station and turned into the driveway where I sat! I slid down in my seat with just the top of my head over the dash. Maybe he'll think this is a lover's car. The lights continued past my location. He must have seen the car. It's now or never.

I started the Dart and eased out without lights. The Pontiac turned left into a large open area that had been bulldozed clear of all trees and undergrowth.

Okay, Buddy, it's me and you, I thought, falling in behind him. He began turning in a large circle. I accelerated and switched on my headlights. Dirt and gravel flew up behind the Pontiac as he tried to outmaneuver me back toward the entrance of the clearing. No way. I had the angle on him and the Dodge would accelerate and maneuver with any vehicle of that time. I hit the siren. With that, he spun the Pontiac in a tight circle and slid to a stop. He was out and running toward the edge of the clearing by the time I got stopped.

My three-cell flashlight in hand, I jumped out of the Dart for yet another foot chase. I loved it. As he approached the edge of the clearing, he went up in the air, then disappeared. I had gained on him quickly across the open ground and found myself headed up a slight embankment. Bulldozers had pushed all the trees and brush to the sides of the clearing and into a deep ravine.

I leaped as I reached the top and it seemed as though I would fall forever. Then WHOMP, "UNGH!" I landed on the back of John Benjamin, who was trying to get up after his own fall. It was black as pitch.

"You're under arrest," I said, knowing by the size of this muscular individual I might be in for a lot of trouble. "I've got him, Koppe!" I called loudly from the hole. If he thought I had a partner with me he would be less likely to give me trouble, I reasoned.

As we climbed back up the embankment, Benjamin looked around. "Where's your partner?" he asked.

"He's probably on the radio in our car. Don't worry about him," I said, placing my handcuffs on his big wrists. I yelled again into the darkness, "There was just one and I got him." Benjamin could still give me trouble.

Now I had two vehicles, one with 182 gallons of moonshine on it, a prisoner and no one to help me. I couldn't leave the liquor car, so I placed Benjamin in my car and sat and waited. Sure enough, in about 15 minutes Koppe called. I gave him my position, and soon he, Frazier and Todd drove up.

I'm sure by this time Benjamin had figured out I was alone all along. He realized my bluff saved him from doing something foolish. One or both of us could have been seriously injured if he had decided to fight. As an old black man once said to one of our agents, "You just got to be there when they're there, be sly like a fox, and you'll catch them every time."

15.

IT'S RED! IT'S RED!

CHECKING A MOONSHINE still was always an exciting experience. We never knew if the moonshiners would be there or if a lookout would be watching. About the middle of May, state revenue agent Bobby Imes called. "I've got information there's a pretty good still in your old territory close to Williamson in Spalding County. You want to send somebody to check it with me?"

"I'll go myself."

"If you'll meet me at the sheriff's office in Griffin, I'll get a deputy to drop us out."

An hour later, Imes and I were walking through the woods. We had dropped out about a mile from where the still was located and were getting close.

"Whoa," Imes whispered as we almost walked out into an open field. "We should hit the workway soon."

Imes was leading the way and when we found the workway he paused to listen for any sounds of activity. Nothing but the sounds of birds and a farm tractor several miles away.

Moving on into the still site, we saw that one of the two 1,500 gallon fermenter stills had recently been run and was hot. It was an above-average operation for that area.

"They'll probably run again in about two days if you want to wait," commented Imes.

"It's your information, but for my part I'd like to catch someone."

"Me too," he agreed.

When I gave the location to Jim Elder that afternoon, his only comment was, "We'll get on it."

Three days later, Elder came into my office. "Frazier and Stanfill checked that still in Spalding County. It'll probably run today. They're on the ground now and Jim Arey and I are going down to help them raid. You wanna go?"

What a question.

"I'll pick up Bobby Imes at the sheriff's office and be on the radio. Give me a call when you're ready and we'll come in by the workway and flush it," I volunteered. I always wanted to flush.

When I got to the sheriff's office in Griffin, Imes was waiting with Deputy Franklin Pitts. I thought, Well, there'll be three of us to flush. No problem.

We had just turned onto the Rover-Williamson Road when the radio came to life. "670, this thing is active—come on in!"

As we approached the farm where the distillery was located, Imes spoke up. "Drop me and Arey at the house—there might be someone there. I'll check it and then follow you on in."

"Good idea."

Pitts and I left Imes and the government car in the back yard and continued on foot down the still workway. It was a beautiful day.

We entered dense woods about 50 yards from the stills and I heard a noise off to my right. Signaling to Pitts to follow me, I found another foot trail and followed it towards the sound. There were 75 cases of one-gallon cola jugs stacked near the path along with several 55-gallon drums of gasoline. I nearly overlooked Tom Ulysses, who was bent over filling the gallon jugs with moonshine from a large steel vat.

Only ten feet from him, I froze and waited. I knew his first reaction would be to break and run so I eased my way toward him. He sensed the movement and stood upright.

"Federal officer—you're under arrest," I said quietly, trying not to excite him into alerting the other still hands. His eyes grew as big as saucers and his hands clawed at the sky.

"Yes, sir!" he gulped.

I had arrested several hundred moonshiners but had never seen one react like this. His eyes were glued on something just over my right shoulder. I glanced back, right into the muzzle of a cocked, nickle-plated .357. If Pitts had fired at the moonshiner from that position it would have burned the hair off the side of my head and deafened me permanently. No wonder Ulysses was bug-eyed. I was, too.

Gently I pushed Pitts' pistol to one side and left the moonshiner in his custody.

"I'll go on in and flush the still," I whispered breathlessly.

I eased back onto the main still path, where I met Imes and Arey. "There's no one at home," Imes said.

"We've already got one jugging up liquor." I motioned towards the side path.

We continued down the main path. The stills were set up on a small creek surrounded by heavy underbrush. The gasoline burner was going strong and liquor was pouring from the radiator condenser.

"CRASH—SPLASH." George Dodge had seen us and was trying to escape.

"Down the creek! Down the creek!" I shouted, warning the other agents of the direction of his flight.

Ten minutes later, Arey and Stanfill returned with Dodge in custody, both claiming to have caught him.

Elder, Frazier, Stanfill, Arey and I spent the remainder of the afternoon setting off dynamite charges and loving every minute of it.

For the next several months, activity remained hot and heavy. I was flying one or two nights a week, trailing liquor vehicles, while Wally Hay and John Guy tried to keep up with information furnished by Jim Daniels, the Eastern pilot. John Crunkleton and the DeKalb County Vice Squad had an informer who was "shucking the corn," and we seized liquor cars almost every night in Atlanta and adjoining DeKalb County.

One night in September, Crunkleton called.

"Charley, we've got some information on a load moving tonight. Can you meet me and Rogers at the Huddle House about six o'clock?"

"I'll be there. I'll bring Jim Elder and another car."

Jim and I met John and Detective Rogers as planned. John briefed us and it was decided that

Rogers would ride with me, and Elder would ride with Crunkleton. Koppe, Harbolt and new agent Mike Gillis would jump the liquor car. The movement was supposed to take place near the intersection of Third Avenue and Memorial Drive.

We all took our positions and at 8:30 P.M. Harbolt called.

"He's headed west on Boulevard Drive. It's a black 1960 Chrysler. Couldn't get the tag number."

I had recently been assigned a yellow and black 1965 Ford hardtop seized from Clarence High on an undercover buy. It had been in storage for over a year and was a good looking, sharp vehicle with low mileage. I hadn't gotten a chance to use it in a chase since giving up my hot-rod Dodge. Although I knew it couldn't perform like the Dodge, I thought maybe I could slip up on them.

Rogers and I turned onto Boulevard Drive and I poured on the coal. We saw Koppe's taillights ahead of us and a vehicle in front of him.

"We're going to pull him over," the radio crackled.

WHRRRRRRRRRRR—Koppe hit his siren as he pulled alongside. The Chrysler pulled over at a 45-degree angle to the curb. Gillis piled out and headed directly towards the driver's door.

SKREEEEECH—the Chrysler suddenly roared backward. Gillis, who was wearing wing tip shoes with steel taps on the heels, slipped on the cobblestones and fell. Thinking the Chrysler had hit him, I floorboarded the Ford. We flashed by Gillis and the other government car. Rogers looked back.

"He's getting up, thank God."

The liquor car roared up Boulevard Drive. I was about four car lengths behind him with my siren wide open. The Ford was doing okay. Rogers stayed on the radio, giving our position. We were coming up on one of Atlanta's major thoroughfares, Moreland Avenue, which always had heavy north-south traffic, even at this time of the evening. We approached the traffic light on Moreland doing 75 and the driver of the Chrysler couldn't stop now if he wanted to. The light was red.

In the excitement of the chase, Rogers had forgotten to let go of the microphone button.

"It's *red!* It's RED! G—damn it's RED!" he screamed.

I don't know if the drivers on Moreland heard the siren or Rogers, or if it was a stroke of fate but both cars careened through the intersection wide open without being hit. I imagine several people had to visit their dry cleaners' the next day.

There was a crown in the center of Moreland Avenue for drainage, and the Chrysler bottomed out. Sparks flew in all directions from under the car.

BAM—we bumped him from behind. Slowed by the sudden jolt, the Chrysler turned right at the next street. I was within a car's length and swung the steering wheel so hard to the right that I almost pulled the left front tire and wheel off the Ford. The hubcap went sailing across someone's front yard.

At the next corner the driver tried to make another right turn. Not quite. He slammed the liquor car up under the front porch of a house. I skidded to a stop and Rogers bailed out of the car.

Usual procedure called for the driver of a chase car to stay with the captured liquor car and the passenger to be the foot chase man. I didn't know Rogers had bad feet. In about fifteen minutes he returned, empty-handed. We later learned that Foots Smith, the driver, had outrun several officers before, both in cars and on foot.

Anyway, we got the car and 16 gallons of moonshine and had a lot of fun doing it. Rogers took a lot of kidding about screaming, "It's red! It's red!" over the airwaves but the next month he came up with information on a 1956 Ford. We caught it hauling 237 gallons. This time Foots didn't get away.

I was always amazed at the amount of moonshine liquor the haulers could fit into an automobile. The old Hudson Hornet would hold 200 or more gallons, but most loads were 150 to 200 gallons, so I was surprised when a week later, we caught a 1960 Pontiac on Bankhead Avenue with 266 gallons of moonshine in half-gallon plastic bottles. They were packed in every open space of the Pontiac, even in the door panels. Olyn Thomas, a north Georgia trip boy, was the driver. He tried to fool us by using a Texas tag, a highly unusual tactic.

The trailing of suspected vehicles on an almost nightly basis continued to pay off. We located a house with a small outbuilding in south Fulton County on Butner Road, a rural farm area. We trailed liquor cars to the house on two different occasions and after following them back into downtown Atlanta, seized one with more than 200 gallons of moonshine. The liquor was warm, indicating that it almost certainly came from a distillery at the house on Butner Road. Although the house and outbuilding didn't seem big enough to contain a large distillery, we obtained a federal search warrant for the premises. On Friday, October 13 we served the warrant.

As we pulled into the yard, Elder, Stanfill and I ran to the house. Harbolt, Koppe and Chet Bryant went directly to the outbuilding. Edith Lane and her husband, Leroy, were arrested after we found moonshine and over a ton of sugar in the house.

In the floor of the outbuilding, the other agents found a trap door leading to a big underground distillery. James White and Robin John were arrested there. They had made more than 330 gallons of moonshine that day and could average that much liquor on a daily basis.

Two trucks and two cars parked in the yard were seized along with several tons of sugar.

The underground covered pit was carefully camouflaged and the moonshiners had positioned a large attic fan to pull fresh air into the hole. The outlet for the fan was in an old junked car sitting over the hole. It was very well concealed and probably would have operated for years if not for the use of the airplane in our surveillance work. It was a hot and stifling place to labor, but as they say, some people will do anything to keep from working for a living.

ATF Agents Frazier, Weems, Chuck Stanfill, Jim Elder and Deputy Franklin Pitts stand on 1,500 gallon groundhog still in Spalding County, Georgia.

ATF Agents Bob Todd, Jim Arey and John Rowden examine junked vehicle used as camouflage over large underground distillery, Fulton County, Georgia.

16.

THE SNIFFER

By late October, 1967, Bill Griffin had been promoted to Assistant Regional Commissioner for Criminal Enforcement in the southeast region. The Chief of Enforcement was Tommy Thompson, and Marvin Shaw was Assistant Chief.

Shaw called me at the district office. "Charley, we've got a so-called super secret weapon being developed to help us locate stills. Do any of our agents have an active still located?"

"If they don't it will be a surprise to me," I said confidently.

"Check on it and come on over to my office about eleven. We'll go to lunch and discuss it with Bill and Tommy."

Here I go again, eating lunch with the brass. Hope I don't drop food in my lap.

Twenty minutes later I was talking to Jim Whitehurst in Newnan. "We have a 1,200-gallon groundhog still we just checked between Carrollton and Villa Rica. It's active!"

"Hold off raiding it until you hear from me. I'll explain later," I said.

When I arrived at the regional office, Pearl Wilder, an ATF legend, greeted me. "Go on in, Mr. Weems, they're waiting for you."

Everyone loved Pearl. She was dedicated to the Lord and to ATF—a fine human being.

Bill Griffin got right to the point. "Charley, we've got a man coming in from California tomorrow to try out some kind of new device to help us locate stills. Do you have an active still we can try it on?"

"Yes, sir."

"All right. This guy's some scientist who's sold Headquarters a bill of goods on his idea. I hope it works. Be here tomorrow morning at nine ready to do whatever the man wants. You wanna go eat lunch with us?"

"I appreciate the offer but I'd better get on down to Newnan and check this still out myself," I begged off.

I stopped by the Varsity and got a couple of hot dogs and a fried peach pie to go. I was a lot more comfortable with that anyway.

The next morning Griffin, Shaw and I met with this very distinguished scientist named Dr. Snyder. He began pulling small round glass culture containers out of his briefcase, explaining that the petri dishes contained a gel of nutrients to feed the microorganism. When subjected to alcohol vapor, even in minute amounts, this microorganism had been found to radiate or react in a way that it could be registered on a very sensitive light meter. The petri dishes would be placed in a small black box containing electrical sensors and a meter on the outside of the box would measure the radiation. If there was no alcohol vapor in the air, the meter would register zero. The higher the content of alcohol vapor, the higher the meter reading. The box was equipped with a small battery-operated fan to pull outside air across the organism, causing the reaction.

Dr. Snyder gave us volumes of technical information about the development of the technique, the sensitive devices and how they worked, and on and on. To me the proof would be in the pudding.

With the professor in tow, I arrived in Newnan at lunchtime. Jim Whitehurst met us at the office.

"Let's go feed this guy some good Georgia barbecue," he suggested.

"Sounds good to me."

The California scientist had a puzzled look on his face. He probably thought people from Georgia ate only possum shanks and crow gizzards as depicted on *The Beverly Hillbillies.*

Reluctantly, he followed our lead and ordered a barbecue plate at Sprayberry's, one of the oldest family-run barbecue restaurants in the south. Soon he was enjoying the hot spicy pork and topping it off with a fried apple pie. From the pleased expression on his face afterward, I believe he was suitably impressed.

Except for large metro areas such as Atlanta, most of the south remained rural, with vast expanses of land comprised of farms and woodland. The area between the small cities of Carrollton and Bremen fell into this category. We headed north on Highway 27 out of Carrollton.

"Turn right at the next dirt road," Whitehurst said suddenly. "Pull into this old church on the right. The still is about a mile from here."

"Don't tell me the direction," Dr. Snyder spoke up quickly. "Let me get this device in operation," he said, starting the fan on the black box.

Jim and I watched closely. A red light came on. The meter fluctuated slightly and settled back on zero.

"We have to be downwind of the alcohol plume in order to pick it up. Let me check the wind." He held another device outside the car window.

"The wind is from the southwest," Snyder stated emphatically, checking a small compass.

This guy came prepared, I thought.

The professor had explained to us previously how the plume of vapor rising from fermenting mash would contain alcohol vapor and would be wafted by air movement for a distance of several miles.

So all we had to do was know where the still was, plus the wind direction, and move downwind of the still to get a reaction from the microorganism. But if you knew where the still was to begin with, what good was this thing?

This was the scientific approach—no more smelling the mash with our noses. No more looking for signs of traffic in the woods with our eyes. No more listening for the sounds of a fuel oil burner with our ears. Here was the answer, all the way from California.

"All right. If you'll just drive around the area of the still remaining about a mile away, I should be able to pick up some reaction on my meter."

Whitehurst was driving and I watched the doctor and the meter intently. The needle quivered occasionally but remained on zero.

After we had made a complete circle, the professor looked puzzled. We parked at the old church again.

"Let me try another one," he said, pulling out a different microorganism, which apparently was the back-up quarterback.

He's putting in the first team—now we'll get results, I thought. Whitehurst raised his eyebrows but said nothing. What did we know about finding stills anyway? As we started out to make the next circle I told Jim to move in closer this time. Still nothing.

"I can't understand it," the professor mumbled.

"Jim, let's walk in to the still and see what happens."

The box humming under the doctor's arm, we walked from a small dirt road into a densely wooded area. The doctor appeared nervous but I assured him there would be no moonshiners at this still. We had been in the area for two hours now and if they were there to begin with, they were long gone.

"Look!" the doctor shouted. The needle had moved about halfway up the scale. The still was some ten yards ahead.

"If we can get this thing within 30 feet of a still we'll be in high cotton," Whitehurst cracked.

The professor didn't think it was funny, but I did. After a few more minutes of experimentation at the still site, the dejected doctor was ready to go. Pete Murphy and John Kreeger met us at Bremen. Whitehurst left with them to go back and destroy the stills. The doctor and I began the long drive back to Atlanta.

He was still tinkering with the machine when we passed through Villa Rica.

"Look—look!" he shouted.

I pulled into a service station. The needle was moving erratically.

"Turn around." The doctor was excited now.

I turned the car around and slowly headed back west on Highway 78, watching the needle on the black box. Suddenly, it moved to the top of the scale and stayed there. I glanced to the right and saw an American Legion Club. After we passed by, the needle retreated to its zero location.

I turned the car around again, and the same thing happened. The microorganism was reacting to all the legal alcohol being consumed at the American Legion post on a Friday night!

Not ready to admit defeat, the doctor mumbled as I dropped him off at his hotel, "Apparently it needs some refinement."

"Right," I said. It worked, but I was absolutely sure we could find an American Legion post without it! But at least ATF had progressed a little since the days of the drip can.

That was the last I ever heard of the sniffer.

☆ ☆ ☆

All police work involves a great amount of waiting and patience. An airline pilot once said, "Flying is hours of boredom punctuated by moments of sheer terror." Police work is like that sometimes.

One day a call came in on the radio. "670, call the Gainesville POD as soon as possible."

When I did, Area Supervisor Bob Scott answered the phone.

"Charley, can you get a plane and meet one of our agents in Anderson, South Carolina by noontime today? I know it's short notice but a load of liquor is supposed to be coming across the Georgia line this afternoon."

"I'll be there as soon as I can. Tell the agent in South Carolina I'll be in aircraft N1689 Foxtrot."

At 12:15, I sat down in Anderson. Agent Bob Clunan met me at the airport.

"You didn't have to rush—I don't think it'll move until after dark."

Now he tells me.

Ten hours later we received a radio call. After some initial confusion, we picked up a large van truck on Interstate 85 heading west. Working with a new observer, especially at night from the air and in heavy traffic is tedious to say the least, but this South Carolina agent soon caught on. We were slow flying at 5,000 feet as the truck crossed the Georgia line, heading southwest towards Atlanta. Once he passed Commerce, he began taking back roads. I kept Bob Scott informed by radio.

When the truck pulled into an old-time bootlegger's yard in Barrow County near Winder, Scott decided to knock it off. I headed back to South Carolina with Clunan and later found out they had made two arrests and seized 360 gallons of moonshine on the truck.

A pretty good night's work.

Typical chicken house used by moonshiners to conceal large illicit distillery in north Georgia.

17.

DAY OF INFAMY

In November, Frankie Waites called downstairs to my office. "Charley, what have you done now?" she asked seriously.

"Huh?"

"Mr. Lane wants to see you in his office." Then, "Ha ha ha ha ha." Frankie's cheerful disposition and infectious laugh made working in the office a pleasure.

"I'll get you back," I said and hung up. I headed upstairs.

"Charley, I've got a detail for you," said Bob Lane. "This year the national office has decided to give new agents from all areas of the country some actual experience on the ground doing surveillance, trailing, preparing warrants, and so on in the Atlanta area. They want us to find some good sites for a stash house and still location and set up a distillery for them to raid. This has been done before to a lesser degree in the Washington area, but this time everything will be taught from the Atlanta regional office. We'll furnish the sites, vehicles and support needed to make the training a success. It's all yours."

"Yes, sir, I'll get on it!"

As I left the office, Frankie was still grinning.

I lived in a small frame house about three miles north of Jonesboro in Clayton County, my home since childhood. When I returned from military service after World War II, my father and I built my house next door to his. My father was killed in an automobile accident directly in front of the place in 1966 and my mother had moved in with me and my family. She never went back to the old house. She had recently passed away and the old house was vacant, as it had been for more than two years. It would make a good stash house for the training program.

The previous year I had purchased a 54-acre farm in an adjoining county. It was beautiful land and I hoped to build there someday after I sold the Clayton County property. The farm in Henry County would be an ideal place to set up a distillery for training the new agents.

The Newnan agents salvaged a complete distillery and for the next two weeks Jim Elder and I worked at getting everything ready. Even though our business was destroying distilleries, we did have some experience in setting them up, having done so at the Southeastern Fair in Atlanta on several occasions. The stills were always a big attraction because people were curious to see how moonshine was made.

I contacted my old friend, Sheriff Hiram Cook in Henry County and told him we would be setting up a moonshine still for training new agents on my farm north of Stockbridge. By the time we got everything ready at the still site there was a well-worn trail to the distillery. Everything was as authentic as we could make it.

The Basic Investigator School involved much more than just surveillance and still work. It ran for several weeks and covered a multitude of subjects, with classroom work in criminal law, photography, firearms laws and arrest procedures, but the most enjoyable part for the new agents was the field exercise.

By the first of December when the field exercise was to begin, everything was ready. Atlanta agents acted as the still hands. Mr. Little, the school director from Washington, later said that it was the best school he ever participated in.

Thursday, December 7 was the wrap-up day for the exercise. The new agents had worked well together, trailing the agent/suspects to the stash house and then to the distillery. They appeared before one of the instructors who was acting as a U.S. Commissioner and secured a search warrant for my old house and made a successful raid. I enjoyed seeing them learn in a realistic setting.

After the exercise was over, about 35 or 40 agents stood around laughing and talking about the raid on the still and subsequent chase of the violators on foot.

"At the last school in Virginia, Warren McConnell, who's over 40 years old, outran every agent there," someone volunteered.

"Shit, if I couldn't outrun a 40 year old man, I'd turn in my badge!" boasted George Nowicki.

I remembered the guy in the Buick calling me "grand paw."

"I don't want your badge, George, but I'm 40 and I'll just give you a chance to outrun me," I said, pulling off my jacket.

Nowicki couldn't back down now. There were too many witnesses and they all began clamoring for a foot race.

"Where can we race?" he asked, looking for a way out.

"There's a pasture in back of the barn."

As we walked toward the barn, I sized up Nowicki. He was at least 15 years younger than I and about 6'2"—he looked as though he could run. I knew he had played end for the University of Georgia football team and was in excellent condition. Maybe I had over-loaded myself this time!

I paced off about 60 yards for a race course.

"No, no, we need to race at least 100 yards," Nowicki insisted.

"Well, if you say so."

We moved back another 40 yards.

"Now, does this suit you?" I asked. I figured I might as well cover myself in case I lost. I could say George chose the distance.

The starter, Glen Brazil, was up at the barn. "When I drop my hand, take off."

Agents crowded on both sides of the finish line.

Brazil's arm dropped and I dug in, getting a little jump on George. After about 20 yards, he pulled alongside. For such a tall man, he was quick!

Working as I did, walking and chasing moonshiners on a regular basis, I was in good shape, too. I weighed 160 and loved to run.

I didn't want any argument or excuses as to who won the race. My pride and adrenalin were pushing me ahead. As we flashed across the finish line, there was no doubt who had won. December 7 was a day of infamy for Nowicki.

For 25 years he has been kidded, especially by Agent Roy Longenecker, about being outrun by a 40-year-old-man, but he was a good sport about it and we became close friends.

After the race, several other young agents challenged me to a foot race, Glen Brazil for one, but I knew when to stop. I had proved my point—no need to keep on and maybe get beaten.

That would take some of the luster off my grandpa image.

ATF Agents Ed Hughes, Weems, Ray Hahn, Satterfield and Phil McGuire, Atlanta, Georgia.

18.

HEARD COUNTY

ARVIN CARTER HAD been on our list of major liquor law violators for some time and was reputed to be the head of a very large moonshine operation. In the last week of January, 1968, the Atlanta and Newnan posts continued their concentration on major violators.

"Jim, let's start at the beginning," I told Elder. "We know where Carter lives. Every time we get caught up a little we'll put someone on the ground to watch his driveway. After we establish a pattern of his movements, we'll start using the plane."

"Sounds good to me," he agreed.

Early one morning we dropped off Emory Sheppard and John Rowden. At the end of the day they gave us a description and tag number of Carter's new white Buick. He had left home and returned on two occasions. We decided continued observation would be productive—if we could find the time.

On February 13, we got our first big break watching Carter's house. Around three-thirty that afternoon the new Buick pulled out with Carter driving.

"670, he's headed west on 78 Highway."

Dale Harbolt and I were waiting with a 172 at Fulton County Airport, not more than ten miles from Carter's house in Douglas County.

"We're on the way," Harbolt advised.

I cranked up the Cessna and got an immediate clearance for takeoff from the control tower. I had visited the tower a number of times and the controllers knew we were federal officers.

"1678 Foxtrot. We'll be westbound at 3,000," I reported to Atlanta Departure Control.

"Roger, 78 Foxtrot, radar contact."

"Do you still have him?" Dale asked the ground units.

Chuck Stanfill answered. "Ten-four, but you need to pick him up as soon as you can. We're almost to Mabelton. He's behind a big black and white tractor trailer."

Highway 78 was just off our left wing and I was flying parallel to it. "Is that him up ahead?" I asked Dale.

"I think so." And to the ground unit, "Did he just pass a Texaco on the right?"

"That's correct," they advised.

"Okay, we have him. You can fall back."

Flying as pilot on aerial surveillance missions was some of the most hectic, tiring, stressful work I've ever done, yet it was some of the most rewarding. One of the primary things that made ATF successful in this new technique was the caliber of our observers. Carl Koppe could recognize by name every street in Atlanta, and could identify every alley from the air, even at night. Ed Michaels was almost as good and

Jimmy Satterfield, Jim Elder, Dale Harbolt, Hugh Merrill, Chuck Stanfill, Frank Lane and Jim Arey all made excellent observers.

Harbolt was one of the many ATF agents who would always come through in a tight situation. He later became an ATF pilot and ironically was killed in Oklahoma City in a tragic accident in an ATF aircraft. He was fearless and even in his last moments tried to maneuver his aircraft away from a residential area.

I miss him still.

As the Buick continued west, Elder and the ground units scrambled to find parallel roads so they could get ahead of Carter.

"We're almost to Villa Rica," Dale reported. "He's stopped at a Shell truck stop east of the city limits. He's going inside."

I began a slow, steady climb to a higher altitude and moved out in a wider circle.

In a few minutes Elder was back on the air. "Looks like there's a high-level meeting going on."

Carter was talking to Bud Corham, a major supplier of sugar and other raw materials, and Richard Black, one of the largest dealers in wholesale moonshine in the south.

"Carter just left headed west on 78. Looks like Black and Corham are headed east in a red and white 1956 Ford. Who do you want to take?"

"We'll stay with Carter," I said and swung the 172 to the west. "You do what you can with the Ford but don't get too close. We can work him the next time."

The Buick turned north on State Highway 101. An hour later we reached Rome, a medium sized city in northwest Georgia.

"He just pulled into a parking lot next to a hardware store," Harbolt pointed out. "He's going inside."

We were on our own with the airplane. The other units were involved with trailing Black and Corham somewhere south of us. Studying the area closely and getting coordinates off the aircraft navigational radios, I made a crude map and notes of the store location.

"He's loading something in the trunk—can't tell what it is." Harbolt had the binoculars on him now.

"All right. We'll just stay with him."

The car headed back south. Why would Carter drive 75 miles to Rome to buy something at a hardware store when he could have gone east just 15 miles to Atlanta where there were an unlimited number of hardware stores? He must be up to something illegal.

The Buick took U.S. 27 south out of Rome through Cedartown, Bremen and Carrollton into Heard County. The plane was running low on fuel and it was almost dark.

"I hope he does something soon." Harbolt had noticed the fuel gauges also.

Franklin, the county seat of Heard County, was just ahead of us. The car slowed and turned into a paved driveway on the right.

"He might be trying to throw off anyone trailing him," I told Dale.

"No, he's going on up to the house. It's a nice brick house—in fact it looks like the nicest one in this town."

We circled for a few minutes to make sure the vehicle was going to remain there for a while, then I headed to the Carrollton airport to get fuel.

When we returned, the car was gone. The place looked too nice to be concealing a still, with the expensive house and being located so close to Franklin, but it needed checking anyway. Carter wasn't just sightseeing.

One of the great advantages of using an airplane in our investigative work was the mobility it afforded us. On the following Friday I spent 13 hours searching for moonshine stills with Air Force pilot-turned-special agent Ed Gray, who was stationed at Swainsboro, Georgia. Ed was one of the first young Air Corps officers to fly a B-17 bomber across the Atlantic to England and participated in more than 25 bombing missions over Germany. He knew something about flying.

I enjoyed Ed's company and although he was hesitant to talk about his flying exploits, I knew he knew more about flying than I would ever learn. Ed and Wally Hay had married sisters so Wally had a close connection with Ed and I liked them both.

Gray and I flew Laurens, Wilkinson, Jones, Jasper, Rockdale, Dodge, Wheeler, Telfair and Treutlen counties and on the way back to Atlanta I checked Henry County. We found several good sites—enough to keep the Dublin and Swainsboro posts of duty busy for a week or so!

Our periodic observations of Arvin Carter continued. Pete Murphy and Bill Barbary walked in and checked the expensive house and the area surrounding it in Heard County. Barbary reported that it was indeed a very expensive home and that there was no distillery anywhere behind the house.

"Did you see anything suspicious at all?" I asked.

"Naw—they're building a big patio out from the rear of the house but I didn't see any signs of a still."

Carter was trailed on various occasions to Atlanta, Douglasville and Bremen. In the middle of March we picked him up again as he left his home in Douglas County. Chuck Stanfill was flying with me. After we took off from Fulton County Airport he crawled over into the back seat.

"We've got him going west," Stanfill reported on the government radio five minutes later.

"Ten-four, we're heading back. Good luck," Elder replied.

It was all ours now. Chuck had flown with me several times before and although he was unfamiliar with some of the area west of Atlanta, he was learning fast and wanted to get in on all the action.

"We'll just see where this gentleman's going today. I hope he surprises us," I remarked.

Just out of Douglasville, Carter turned south on Georgia 5 paralleling the Chattahoochee River in its southward trek to the Gulf of Mexico.

"Looks like he's headed back to Heard County," Stanfill commented.

I was deep in thought. "If he goes back to that same house, there's got to be something there. He has met with Bud Corham in Bremen. Bud's been seen south of Carrollton and is notorious for supplying huge illegal distilleries with sugar and other materials. There's something going on, and I believe the house near Franklin is the key," I mused aloud.

At Roopville the car turned south on U.S. 27.

"Maybe he's got a girlfriend at that house," Chuck surmised.

"Could be."

The car passed the driveway to the house.

"He's going on by."

"Just keep your eye on him." I didn't want to lose him now.

In the edge of Franklin, the vehicle turned into a service station and without stopping, made a complete circle around the station. It stopped at the highway.

"Chuck, he's checking to see if anyone's following him. I think he's getting ready to go back."

"Yeah, he's headed back the way he came. This looks good."

This time the car whipped into the driveway and reached the cover of the wooded area leading to the house in seconds. I eased the Cessna into a shallow turn away from the area. Chuck's binoculars were trained on Carter.

"He's going into the house."

"I've seen enough," I said, continuing northeast towards Atlanta. "It's got to be in that house."

Two months had passed since we first trailed Carter to the house. It was time for action. The next morning I called Jim Whitehurst at Newnan. "How about meeting me at the Newnan airport about eight tonight?"

"I'll be there," Jim replied.

That night, I told Whitehurst that we needed to check the Heard County house again.

"I'll go myself this time," he said.

Two days later Whitehurst called. He said that the large patio out back was finished, but there was no sign of any illegal activity.

The remaining weeks in March we began to really concentrate on Carter. I had to attend federal court on several cases, but every available hour was spent in observing and trailing Carter. We trailed him on two more occasions to Rome where he left a one and a half-ton truck at the rear of a farmer's market. We notified Rome agents Jim Harmon and Joe Burton, but they were too busy with their own investigations to spend much time watching a parked truck.

Meanwhile, Jim West was working on a major violator in the Winder and Athens area named Chauncey Harris. Harris was a notorious major liquor law violator involved in everything from car theft to murder. Using the airplane we trailed Harris and others in Barrow, Gwinnett and Jackson counties, frequently at night.

In spring and summer, thunderstorms are commonplace in the south due to the high temperatures and humidity of the day and the cooling that takes place at night. Pilots who have been lucky enough to survive flying into a thunderstorm never did it again.

One night Hugh Merrill and I took off from Winder at about ten o'clock and were soon orbiting over a suspect's house trailer. West was on the ground. I could see heavy lightning flashing in the southwest and knew it was headed in our direction.

Atlanta Radar reported that a line of thunderstorms was just west of Atlanta and moving to the east at about 30 knots.

"Time to go home," I told Hugh. "Jim, we're going to have to head on in. Looks like some heavy weather moving in from the west."

There was a long pause, then West's voice on the radio. "How about staying another hour? He should move soon."

I tried to explain. "If we don't leave now we won't be able to get back into Atlanta tonight."

"Well, just stay another 30 minutes, then," he persisted.

"We're going in. I'll talk to you tomorrow." I laid the Cessna on its side and headed towards the airport beacon at Winder. I dropped Hugh off and barely made it back to Peachtree-DeKalb before the leading edge of the squall line hit.

About a week later, I met West at the Winder airport. "I'll have to go with you tonight," he said. "No one else showed up."

It was a beautiful summer night, and soon we were flying over the suspected area of activity. I pulled the engine back to 1,700 r.p.m. and lowered the flaps 20°. The airspeed dropped to between 55 and 60 and the stall warning horn would occasionally beep when we hit an air pocket. I could tell West was a little apprehensive, but he said nothing.

After a couple of hours I noticed a few flashes in the east. I knew it was lightning but it was probably close to the South Carolina line, about 70 miles away. I didn't say anything. Soon the flashes became more numerous and quite bright, lighting up the eastern sky. It was about one in the morning and I could see no problem to the south or west toward Atlanta, so I continued to circle.

West had suddenly become very quiet. Finally he could hold it in no longer.

"Is that lightning, Charley?"

"Yeah," I answered casually.

He said nothing. As the sky lit up more and more, I could feel the airplane move as West shifted around on the back seat. Let him squirm, I thought. Maybe next time I tell him I've got to pull off because of thunderstorms he won't argue.

Ten minutes later, West spoke again. "I don't think he's going to move tonight. We might as well go on in."

"We've been staying till two. Let's fly around for another hour, anyway." I was enjoying every minute. I continued circling slowly.

Ten minutes later—"I've got to meet an informer at two. We'll have to go on in," West said, one eye still on the lightning in the east.

I had had enough fun and made my point, so I headed for the Winder beacon.

★ ★ ★

Although Jim West was apprehensive about thunderstorms, he certainly showed no fear of Harris or his associates. One was a brutal killer named Billy Sunday Birt, who became a member of the Harris gang in 1968.

Ruth Harris, Chauncey's mother, was the leader of this group of car thieves, murderers and moonshiners who operated in northeast Georgia and western South Carolina. They were ruthless, violent and persistent law breakers. Ruth's lieutenants were her son Chauncey and her brother "Rooster."

Billy Birt was the enforcer. He boasted on several occasions about killing 52 people. Several of the murders he recounted were verified and he was later convicted of killing a young couple and their two children.

During the time West was investigating this group, they put a price on his head. Birt planned on two different occasions to kill West but fate intervened, and thank God he was not successful.

The Harris gang also put the word out that they were going to burn West's house. One afternoon that fall, Jim West pulled his car into Chauncey's yard. When Chauncey walked up to the car he could see a sawed-off 12 gauge shotgun lying on the seat beside West.

"Chauncey, I understand you're going around telling everyone you're going to burn my house and that Billy Birt is going to kill me. Is that true?"

"No, sir, Mr. West. I never said nothing like that. No sir!"

"Well, I just wanted you to know that you and Billy Birt know where to find me and I'll certainly be glad to accommodate you and anyone else you want to bring along," Jim said, laying his hand on the shotgun.

"No, sir, I didn't say nothing like that!" Chauncey was visibly shaken. No one ever burned West's house.

The criminals ATF agents had to deal with in those years were not all innocent hillbillies making a "little drinking whiskey" as depicted in most folklore.

Working with West every chance I got, we trailed Harris's vehicles and gang members to several large distilleries in the fall of 1970 and the spring and summer of '71. During this time, West developed enough evidence to send most of this notorious gang to the federal penitentiary.

Later, Birt did kill a key witness in the case West had developed against the Harris gang. The story of this gang would fill a book all its own.

House in Heard County, Georgia where distillery was located, 1968.

3000-square foot patio used to conceal huge illicit distillery adjacent to house in Heard County, Georgia.

Charley Weems examines mash in some of the 220 steel drum fermenter barrels, Heard County, Georgia.

Trap door in patio leading into illicit distillery, Heard County, Georgia.

ATF Agents Tommy Stokes, Bill Barbary and David Greer destroy portion of 2,260 gallons of moonshine, Heard County, Georgia.

Triple radiator condensers used at Heard County distillery.

Large camouflaged distillery in swamp, Panhandle section, Clayton County, Georgia.

Close-up of illicit distillery on platform in swamp, Clayton County, Georgia.

ATF Pilots Wally Hay, Marshall Reece, Weems and Bill Ivey.

ATF Agents Jim Berry, Weems, Jim King, Miles Keathley, M.L. Goodwin and Russell Trickey.

Bill Griffin, Ed Hughes, Weems, Berry, Tommy Thompson and Marvin Shaw accept trophy for win at regional pistol match.

Charley Weems accepts payment on $1 bet from Bill Richardson after Regional Pistol Team wins pistol match.

Agents examine Banks County distillery. Note fuel oil burner and moonshine whiskey stacked on left side.

Banks County distillery showing condenser barrel and whiskey catch vat on left.

ATF Agents Elder, Rowden, Weems and Chuck Connor discuss the raid on distillery in Banks County, Georgia.

1956 Ford hot rod caught in chicken house distillery, Banks County, Georgia.

19.

SECRET WEAPON

OUR SURVEILLANCE OF Arvin Carter was interrupted in April of 1968 when the presidential campaigns of both political parties began to heat up. ATF agents were assigned all over the nation to assist the U.S. Secret Service, which simply did not have enough manpower to provide security for all the presidential and vice-presidential candidates. The first week in April, Vice-President Hubert Humphrey made several appearances in Atlanta. A number of Atlanta and Newnan agents spent two days on this security detail. It was new to most of us but was an interesting break from the routine.

On Friday, April 19 after two Newnan agents went in again on the ground at the Heard County house and reported no suspicious activity, I had to see for myself. I couldn't believe Arvin Carter would continue to meet people like Bud Corham every two weeks in west Georgia and take evasive routes back to this house if nothing illegal was going on.

"Jim, I need some help tonight." I called to Elder as he was leaving the branch office squad room.

"Sure. Do we need anyone else?" he asked.

"No. If you'll pick me up about nine tonight at my house, I'll explain to you then. How about bringing the old Ford pickup we use for surveillance sometimes."

"I'll be there."

While most men were out with their wives having dinner on this Friday night, I was sitting on the porch anxiously awaiting Elder's arrival so I could get back to work. Most ATF agents were like that. That's one reason the divorce rate is so high among law enforcement personnel.

As Elder drove through the darkness toward Newnan I told him about the recent observations of the Heard County location and that they had not uncovered anything suspicious.

"I'm not trying to find fault with the Newnan agents, but I'll never be convinced this house is not a distillery location or a huge stash of liquor until I see for myself."

Elder nodded in agreement.

"Jim, you and I are going to check it. No one knows we're in the area. If we find there's nothing there, we won't mention going in. If it is there, we'll get enough probable cause for a search warrant and everyone will be happy."

From the air I had seen an old sawmill road leading off one of the secondary roads in the area. Elder turned in, switched off the headlights and guided the old pickup slowly about a mile back into the woods.

"We'll leave the truck here," I said. It was eleven o'clock and there was still some moonlight left, but I knew the Moon would be going down in about two hours. I figured it would take us an hour of steady walking to get to the highway across from the house. Sure enough, a little after midnight we broke out of the woods. We recognized the area and located the house just as the Moon was disappearing over the horizon. The night grew very dark.

"Let's just watch for a while and see what happens," I whispered.

By one o'clock only an occasional car or truck would pass on the highway. The house was hidden from us behind some trees but I could see a faint glimmer from a light in one of the rooms.

"Let's ease on in," I whispered to Jim.

We crossed the highway, two shadows drifting across in the darkness. We were both dressed in dark green work clothes and green Browning boots. ATF agents perfected Stealth techniques before the military even thought of them.

I felt my way along the shoulder of the highway and found another old sawmill road. The house was located on a knoll and was surrounded on the north and west sides by a swampy area. The sawmill road led up the side of a hill overlooking the water on the north.

Moving in close to a residence late at night is very demanding and dangerous, especially in rural areas where people usually shoot first and ask questions later. Halfway up the hill and even with the house, Elder and I stopped to watch and listen for anything unusual. It was deathly quiet.

Mmmmmmm—I could hear a very faint but steady hum.

"Do you hear that?"

"Hear what?" Elder asked.

"It's down here," I whispered, leading the way silently down the hill toward the sound. Reaching the base of the hill, I felt water coming up over my boots. I waded slowly, pausing after each step to listen. Soon we were up to our knees in water.

Georgia swamps are noted for their snakes, especially cottonmouth moccasins. A cottonmouth is one snake that looks for trouble and will not run away. There were also copperheads and an occasional rattlesnake, but we didn't have time to worry about snakes.

The sound was just ahead now. We had almost reached the base of the knoll, about 150 feet from the house. I felt in front of me, trying to find the source of the humming noise. My hand touched a wooden box. I leaned down close and suddenly realized that the hum was coming from an electric water pump inside. They sure aren't pumping water out of this swamp for drinking or bathing. There's a big still somewhere close, I thought.

Elder and I slowly and silently retraced our footsteps back to the old road.

"It's in there," I whispered.

He nodded.

The old road was grown up with large bushes and gave us an excellent vantage point from which to observe the house and patio. I peered through the darkness. The patio seemed as big as the house.

"Do you smell it?" Elder had picked up the odor of mash.

"I do now. Let's ease around to the side of the house."

A faint glimmer of light flickered in the wall. A big attic fan was mounted in the wall of the patio foundation to furnish ventilation, and light from inside shone between the turning blades. The still's got to be under the patio, I thought.

"Jim, we've got enough to get a search warrant— we'd better ease out." Our two months' surveillance of Carter was about to pay off.

I called Whitehurst. The next morning when I arrived at the Newnan office, all the agents were there.

I explained what I had found the night before. Emory Sheppard and I drove back to Franklin in the '65 Ford hardtop. We carefully noted the mileage from the city limit sign north to the driveway leading to the house, then wrote out a detailed description of the house and premises so there would be no question as to the validity of the warrant. We returned to Newnan where a judge was waiting with Whitehurst and obtained a federal search warrant. Now we were ready.

It was decided that we would maintain 24-hour observation of the still house until the seizure was made. Two agents would go in that night to begin surveillance. I finally got home at three o'clock Saturday afternoon.

At eight o'clock Sunday morning I headed back to Heard County. I heard Elder and Chester Bryant on the government radio. Hobbs and Barbary were on the ground and reported seeing little activity.

Whitehurst and J.P. Lott were parked in a sawmill road about two miles from the observation post.

We watched the still house round the clock for five days. On Wednesday, just after midnight, Emory Sheppard and I pulled up behind a big cargo van driven by one of Bud Corham's trip boys, just north of Franklin on Highway 17. I passed and was glad we were in the Ford. Maybe we hadn't been spotted.

Two days later, Bud pulled into a dead end road about two miles from the still site and surprised agents West and Whitehurst. There were no raw materials or liquor on his car, so they had to let him go.

It was time to hit the house. We had been seen in the area too many times and Corham and Carter were no fools. We had seen enough to identify the two still hands and two of the vehicles used to work the still.

On April 25 Barbary called from the observation post. "Looks like they're leaving the house." As it happened there was no one close by with a vehicle. By the time we arrived, the car had disappeared.

"Barbary, you and Stokes cover the north side. We're going in," I called.

With that, we wheeled up the long concrete driveway. The house was deserted. The residents had left in a hurry. There were fresh groceries on the kitchen counter and clothes all over the place.

"Let's see what's under that patio!" I said, to no one in particular. The room under the patio was 75 by 40 and covered 3,000 square feet. It was completely filled with mash barrels, stills and distilling equipment. There was more than 12,000 gallons of mash and

2,260 gallons of moonshine in plastic jugs. They were using 55-gallon steel drums as fermenters—220 of them—and had soldered together three truck radiators as a condenser. It was an elaborate outfit and we managed to seize it before any whiskey left the premises.

It was the largest seizure of a moonshine distillery ever made in Heard County. The distillery room was added onto the rear of the house and made to look like a patio from a distance. Fumes from the distillery were dissipated by the exhaust fan mounted in one wall, which pulled the fumes out over a pan of Clorox. Spent mash was pumped into the swampy area in back.

We had worked for three months using aircraft and ground surveillance, starting from scratch. What had begun as a part-time surveillance ended with the seizure of one of the largest and most elaborate illegal liquor operations in the country, involving two of the most sought-after major liquor law violators. We collected enough evidence to arrest the four people who ran the distillery and Jim West had enough to wind up the conspiracy case he had initiated on Bud Corham and Arvin Carter.

West doggedly worked for another two months tying all the loose ends together and we were successful in sending three people to the penitentiary, one a major violator. The woman who was living on the still received a probated sentence.

No testimony or mention of the use of aircraft was made, nor was it suspected by the moonshiners. For years this was the best-kept secret in ATF—even from Headquarters!

★ ★ ★

By July, the presidential campaigns were starting to heat up. Candidate George Wallace came to Atlanta and with several other agents, I assisted the Secret Service in providing security for Wallace at the Atlanta City Auditorium.

The first of August, 1968, most of the ATF agents in the southeast were told to report to Miami, Florida to assist Secret Service agents in providing security for the participants of the Republican National Convention.

We reported for duty on the morning of August 1 aboard the *U.S.S. Fremont* , an old World War II troop ship. This brilliant money-saving idea came from someone in the Treasury Department. They were not the ones who would have to live in the cramped hold of an antiquated troopship in the sweltering August heat of Miami. It might have been bearable if we could have dressed casually without having to worry about sweating like horses in suits and ties. We were required to eat in the mess hall on the ship—that, too, supposedly would save the government some money.

A typical day was to get up at 6:00 A.M., shower, make our way to the mess hall, eat in shifts, then shower again because we were already wet with sweat, then dress in white shirt, suit and tie. By the time we got down the gangplank onto the dock, sweat was running off us in streams. Then it was time to drive in rush-hour traffic to the huge convention center and receive our assignments.

As long as we could stay inside, we could keep cool. The days all consisted of 12 to 14 hours of duty. Some of the agents guarded particular candidates and others like myself were on duty inside the convention hall all day. My post was on the right side of the podium. I could see the entire convention hall from this prime location near the candidates.

Every morning as we made our way to the mess hall we had to walk through a narrow companionway past the head. The commodes stood in a row along one bulkhead of the ship, with wash basins on the other. There were no partitions to screen the commodes from the open doorway. As we passed every morning there would be two or three agents sitting there looking embarrassed. Chuck Connor, a fine ATF agent and one of the funniest men who ever lived, would always stick his head in the door, wave and tell the poor embarrassed souls there, "Hi, gang! How about giving us a courtesy flush!" Chuck's ribald sense of humor always made things go easier.

After three days and nights on that sweat box of a troopship, several of us found a small efficiency apartment not far from the convention center and rented it. We were told by our supervisors (who were assigned comfortable officers quarters top side) that we had to stay on the ship when off duty, but there was so much confusion and crowding no one knew we weren't sleeping on the ship. Getting any sleep in those holds was impossible anyway. The lights were always on and someone was coming or going all night long. At least we got some rest at the apartment, although it cost us. Once again, ATF agents used improvisation to get the job done properly.

I've never been very impressed with politicians, but while I was there I did get to meet Senator Everett

Dirksen, a man I had admired from afar for a long time. He was a fine gentleman and a true patriot.

Despite the uncomfortable accommodations, it was an exciting and interesting time for most of us but when the convention ended without mishap we were all glad to leave.

★ ★ ★

ATF agents were the most productive federal law enforcement agents in the country, but they occasionally found themselves involved in hilarious situations.

In 1972 ATF agents were once again assigned to Presidential candidate security details all over the country. It was a change from the rugged outdoor situations the adventurous agents faced on a daily basis. After a week or two of following a politician around to fund-raising functions attended by other politicians and wealthy citizens, the agents would become a little tired of all the falderol. To pass the time some of them would engage in a little innocent fun.

Agent Hugh Merrill was on a security detail for Senator Morris Udall, who was campaigning for the presidential nomination. Hugh had been with the Senator and his entourage for some time when they traveled to the Detroit area. As the Senator's convoy wound through the country-club atmosphere of a very affluent area, Hugh was thinking about the mountains of north Georgia. Hugh tells it this way:

"This was one of those places you have to stick a card into the gate to get into the street or the neighborhood. When we arrived at this big mansion, I believe it was the mayor or police commissioner's house, the Senator and his advisors went into a large room to talk politics with about ten influential men from the area.

"We were told we could wait in the kitchen where we were provided sandwiches, coffee and fruit. I ate a sandwich or two and then noticed a big bowl filled with the largest, most beautiful bananas I had ever seen. They must have been ten inches long. I hadn't had a banana in a long time. I decided to get one but I was full of sandwiches and had no place to put it.

"I had a clip on my pistol, so I just took it out of the holster and clipped it on my belt under my coat on the left side. I stuck this huge banana in my holster and pulled my suit coat over it. After about 30 minutes the Senator was ready to go and we drove to a radio station in the area. Udall was to tape an interview to be broadcast at a later time and the security detail was again left outside in the hall.

"I was standing there by myself when this fellow walked up. I guess he worked for the radio station— he had about 15 or 20 pens and pencils in his pocket— and he began talking to me. He asked me about my work.

'I'll bet you've got an interesting job,' he ventured.

'Yeah, it's very interesting.'

'I'll bet it's dangerous.'

'Well, not too bad,' I said modestly.

'Of course, I guess you go well prepared.'

"That's when the bell rang in my head and I began thinking about the banana in my holster. I said, 'Yeah, we're always well prepared.'

"He said, 'What kind of weapon do you carry—well, I don't guess I should ask you that. It's probably a secret.'

'Yeah, it's top secret, the kind of weapon we carry, but if you won't tell anybody, I'll show you.'

'No, no, I won't tell anyone.' He was getting excited. I began to look up and down the hall. He looked also to make sure no one else would see what I was about to show him.

'If you'll lean over here I'll show you what we carry.'

"By now he couldn't wait and as I pulled my coat back and revealed the huge banana in my holster, his eyes grew as big as saucers. He was speechless. He had the most astonished look on his face I have ever seen. The expression on his face when it finally dawned on him I was carrying a banana in my holster broke me up. I began to laugh and then he began to laugh. We were both hysterical when one of the Senator's aides burst out of the studio. 'Keep the noise down. The Senator's taping an interview.'

"He was dead serious, but neither I nor the poor innocent man with the 20 pencils could control our laughter. The aide hustled the poor man into a back room and closed the door. I could still hear him laughing behind the door. I left the building and waited in the parking lot with tears streaming down my cheeks."

It broke the monotony, and I'm sure the radio station man never forgot the day he saw the secret weapon carried by a federal agent guarding a potential President of the United States.

20.

LEARN AND LIVE

ONE AFTERNOON IN May, Carolyn Welch called on the government radio.

"Six-seventy, Mr. Elder wants you to meet him in Griffin at the sheriff's office."

"Ten-four."

The area south of Atlanta was my old territory. As I passed the main Atlanta airport, I thought of the thousands of times I had driven this same stretch of highway. Things had changed drastically since the 1930's.

I was lost in thought when suddenly, the old Spalding County Jail loomed in front of me. Elder was just pulling into the parking lot with state agents Randall Johnson and Bobby Imes.

"Randall's got information on a big outfit north of here. I'll let him tell you," Elder said.

Johnson came right to the point. "We rode through the area earlier today. Looks like they're working it through the yard of a tenant house. The driveway's worn out. It's about two miles south of Luella, and it's supposed to be running every day."

"Sounds good. How do you want to work it, Randall?"

"Bobby can drop us out. He knows a good place to park the car. You and Jim and I will walk in."

"Let's eat first," Elder suggested. We all agreed. We never knew how long we would have to go without food, lying on a big still. Water was never a problem, as there was always a small stream or creek near the still. We seldom worried about drinking from them as long as the water was running. Occasionally we would find cow manure or a dead animal upstream but it didn't seem to have any lasting effect on our health.

We enjoyed some Melear's barbecue and at seven o'clock that evening, Elder, Johnson and I slipped out of my Ford hardtop and hit the woods. Imes would park the car behind a small church about a mile away and wait. Johnson led the way and when we reached the workway we all stopped to listen. Not a sound. They've probably left, I thought.

We continued cautiously down the worn-out trail. This had to be a big one. We eased silently into the still yard. A 1961 Chevrolet pickup was parked to one side and a large portion of the yard was covered with something white. When we got closer I realized there were several hundred one-gallon plastic jugs on the ground, all of them full of moonshine. The truck was loaded and ready to go.

"They're through working today," I whispered, "but it looks like they'll be back for the whiskey sometime tonight."

"Do you want to wait them out?" Johnson asked.

"You bet," Elder answered.

We started to split up to get around the still yard. I had an idea.

"Hold on. I'm going to take the distributor rotor out of the truck. Then if they try to escape in it, it won't start."

"Good idea," both agreed.

I remembered agent Gene Howell's death at the hands of moonshiners escaping from a distillery in a truck several years earlier.

With the rotor in the pocket of my field jacket, I felt a little more secure. "We'll let them get in the truck and then hit it."

"Sounds good."

We split up and I leaned up against a small oak tree at the edge of the still yard. This reminded me of a story about ATF Agent Duff Floyd, an old timer who worked for years out of the Jasper, Georgia Post of Duty. This was one of the most prolific moonshining areas in north Georgia and Duff was a legend among ATF agents and moonshiners alike. He was well known for his kindness, superb woodsmanship and marvelous sense of humor.

Duff had received information on a moonshiner operating in a remote area of Gilmer County. He and Agent Warren Cagle located the still in a laurel thicket in one of the many hollows of the mountains, not far from the beginning of the Appalachian Trail.

After determining that the still would operate sometime that day, Floyd and Cagle set up camp several hundred yards away. Soon they began to hear noises from the still site—"Thump"—"Bump"—and the low roar of a gravity-fed gasoline burner.

"We'll give them time to get the liquor running," Duff said quietly.

An hour later, Duff sent Cagle around to the other side of the still yard with instructions to wait for him to flush. Duff began a slow, step-by-step approach to the still. He spotted a huge oak tree in the edge of the still yard and near the workway. He knew that if he could get behind that tree without being seen, he would have a clear view of the still and the moonshiners.

Slowly and steadily he moved forward. The activity at the still had picked up and he didn't have to worry so much about sounds now.

Reaching the big oak, Duff peered into the still yard. Jeeter Odom and Nozzle Nose Bascum were jugging up moonshine as it poured from the radiator condenser. Occasionally Jeeter would take a sample swallow.

"G—damn," he would gasp. "That's good!"

Duff was enjoying the show.

The more samples Jeeter consumed, the more vocal he became. Nozzle Nose continued to work.

"Hey, you know we're about through. If Duff Floyd is going to catch us, he better get his ass in the road," Jeeter mused. "I think I'll call him up." With that he weaved his way over to the big oak where Duff was hiding. Reaching up on the side of the tree, he began cranking the handle of an imaginary telephone.

"RINGGG—RINGGG," Jeeter sang out gleefully, his hand making circles next to the tree. "Hello—Duff Floyd? This is Jeeter Odom. Me and old Nozzle Nose are out here running my still and we're about ready to leave. If you're going to catch us you better get your ass in the road! Good luck!"

Jeeter was laughing so hard tears were streaming down his cheeks and Nozzle Nose joined in, laughing hysterically.

Duff could hardly restrain himself. Regaining his composure, he calmly stepped from behind the big oak.

"Is this fast enough for you boys?"

Jeeter was stunned. His knees buckled. Nozzle Nose sat down, and the tears of joy turned to tears of sadness.

Duff had the last laugh after all.

"RMRRRR—RRRRR—RRRRR" brought me back from my reverie. Someone had slipped in and was trying to start the Chevrolet pickup. I had to move fast. I bolted toward the truck.

"RMRRRR—RRRRR—RRRRR."

I hit the door and reached into the window on the driver's side. Stew Kelly scrambled to get out of the passenger side. I got a grip on the back of his shirt and as he pulled me through the open window and into the cab, I managed to get my other arm through the window and hold on. Just then Randall Johnson ran up to the other side of the truck and helped me get Kelly calmed down.

In a few minutes, Elder came out of the woods with Arnold Willis in custody. We spent the next two hours pouring out 500 gallons of moonshine and destroying the four 1,300-gallon fermenter stills. We seized the pickup and a 1959 Plymouth that was parked on the workway.

There's an old saying, "you live and learn." In law enforcement it's the reverse—you learn and live.

★ ★ ★

The next week, Sheriff Hiram Cook called. "Charley, how about meeting me at the Henry County Work Camp around noontime tomorrow. We'll eat lunch and go check out some information."

"I'll be there."

Just as I was hanging up the phone, Chuck Lowe walked by my office.

"Chuck, how would you like a free meal at the Henry County Prison Camp tomorrow?"

"Sounds good to me."

"Wear your woods clothes and meet me at the prison camp in McDonough."

"I'll be there," he replied.

There was no need to go into detail—Chuck and I both had been told all we needed to know for now.

The next day, as I drove to the area of the old chain gang camp I began to recall the days of the 1930's, 40's and 50's, when it was common to see prisoners with leg irons and chains working on the public roads. In Gilmer County they pounded huge boulders into small stones to be used on the county roads. In those days serving time, especially at hard labor, meant just that. Prisoners had no air-conditioned cells or televisions and needed no recreational facilities. They got plenty of exercise outdoors. The food was plain. In every prison camp where I ate there was plenty of food and it was nourishing and well prepared, even without a special dietitian!

Sheriff Cook was waiting for us, and after a good meal we headed south toward Locust Grove. About seven miles outside McDonough, Hiram turned onto a well-used dirt road. We passed an old farmhouse sitting well back from the road.

"The still's supposed to be worked through the yard of that house. I'll drop you and Chuck out and pick you up in about two hours at the same place. Be careful," Hiram warned.

"We will," I replied, sliding out of the car about a half-mile from the farmhouse. "If we're not back in two hours give us another hour."

Chuck and I hit the woods.

We soon found the still, which was a big one for that area. It had recently been operated.

"We'll leave it till next week," I told Lowe.

We told the sheriff what we found, and decided to come back five days later.

On July 25, Lowe, Chuck Stanfill and I dropped out and slowly made our way back into the area.

"I hear it," whispered Stanfill.

"Sounds like a vehicle coming in," added Lowe.

"You know where the workway is," I told Lowe. "You and Stanfill cover this side and I'll work my way around to the other side. Just don't let them get in that vehicle and leave. Give me about 15 minutes to get in position and then you can flush."

I knew both agents were anxious to make the initial move. I had made more than my share, so they could have that privilege today.

I inched my way through the underbrush into the edge of the still yard and crawled in among the four

800-gallon wood and aluminum fermenter vats. Three men were working hard, pouring whiskey into one-gallon glass and plastic jugs, then loading the filled jugs into the back of an old Ford station wagon. They were much too busy to notice me watching. I recognized one of them, George Dodge, but didn't know the others.

"Federal officer!" Lowe shouted. Stanfill came charging into the still yard. All three of the moonshiners broke for cover. Dodge bolted towards a hill with me right on his heels. He turned left into a swampy area. I plunged into the swamp water up to my waist and was able to get my hand into the back of his belt and hang on. I had arrested Dodge before. After the initial fright he calmed down.

Wet and muddy, I took him back into the still yard. Lowe and Stanfill had caught the other two.

"Why is it I'm always the one who has to chase his man into a swamp?" I asked good-naturedly.

Lowe and Stanfill just grinned at each other.

We spent the rest of the afternoon setting off C-4 explosions and eating Vienna sausage and crackers we found at the still.

They had to be destroyed some way.

Fire in the Hole!

In January of 1968, we had begun to obtain large amounts of C-4 plastic explosives, detonation cord, caps and fuses from the U.S. Army at Ft. McPherson, Georgia. C-4 replaced the use of dynamite and was available through the military at no cost to ATF. It was also much safer than dynamite to handle and transport. ATF agents naturally became proficient in its use and in no time were blowing illegal distilleries to high heaven with C-4.

Through experimentation each agent determined the proper amount for different size stills. Rarely did they use too little. The sounds of explosions reverberating through the woods gave the moonshiners something to talk about.

On one occasion in south Georgia, some overzealous agents decided to blow up some propane gas tanks—not a wise decision. Who knew the ends would blow off, sending the 90-pound steel tanks rocketing through the woods with fire spewing behind?

"Look *out,*" one of the agents screamed, plunging into the creek. Luckily, no one was hurt, but the resulting fire burned for days before the Forestry Service could put it out.

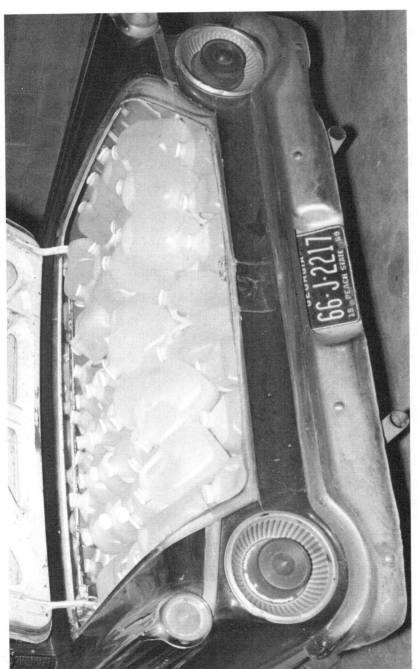

1959 Ford containing 311 gallons of moonshine seized in Atlanta, Georgia.

21.

PERRY BLOOM

PERRY BLOOM'S ORGANIZATION was one of the largest moonshine operations in the country. He, like J.R. Turner, had cultivated numerous law enforcement contacts and sources of information. Catching him would be a major coup.

The office phone rang.

"Mr. Weems, it's Mr. Thompson." Carolyn Welch called from the outer office.

"Yes, sir," I said as I picked up the receiver.

Tommy Thompson, the Chief of Enforcement for the Southeast Region, was a no-nonsense supervisor.

"Come over to my office in about an hour. I've got something for you to do."

An hour later, I walked into Mr. Thompson's outer office and was greeted by Pearl Wilder. "Go on in, Mr. Weems. He's expecting you."

"Charley, the North Carolina agents have been trying to locate one of Perry Bloom's outfits for several weeks now with no success. They think that their radio traffic is being monitored. I understand that you have some radios you squirreled from Headquarters to use in airplanes that aren't on our regular frequencies."

"Yes, sir." No need to lie about it. A friend in Washington had helped me get these so-called experimental radios for use on a limited basis. We had some problems with violators monitoring our frequencies, especially the radio traffic from the airplane because the signal was so strong it could be heard for 20 or 30 miles. Thompson understood. He had probably done a little squirreling of equipment in his days as a field agent, too.

"Call Special Agent Jim Lancaster in Goldsboro, North Carolina, and set it up. Take the radios and a plane and stay as long as they need you. I've already talked to Bob Lane."

"Yes, sir," I said. I left humming my theme song, "On the Road Again," under my breath. I called Lancaster that afternoon.

On Monday morning, I left Gunn Airfield in 2889 Lima, a Cessna 172. Four hours later I arrived at the Goldsboro airport just north of Seymour Johnson Air Force Base, one of the main SAC bases for B-52's. You always had to be especially watchful for those "big mamas" when flying in that area. Jim Lancaster was waiting for me at the airport.

Once again I would be flying with a guy who had ten times my experience and qualification as a pilot, yet I would be pilot in command. Jim had flown the Vought F4U Corsair in the Navy—one of the most advanced fighters of its time and a horse of an airplane. Jim had lost a finger when one flipped over as he was landing it, so he was one of three 3-fingered agents in North Carolina. All were excellent agents even though they were missing one digit.

Joe Carter would be directing the ground surveillance team in the Bloom investigation. He picked up two of the Ultra-high frequency radios and left to join another unit. Lancaster and I took off in the plane and established contact with the ground units.

"Stay well clear of the area until we see some movement," Joe warned.

We climbed up to 8,500 feet. Lancaster made himself comfortable in the back seat. It might be a long night.

By now we were flying over the city of Wilson. I checked in with Seymour Johnson AFB on radar and gave them my altitude. I didn't want a B-52 blowing my doors off if I could help it.

At 7:00 P.M. Joe called. "He's loading at the warehouse."

Jim had briefed me on the layout of the area and we had no problem finding the truck.

Jim was watching through binoculars. "We'll probably need to drop down a little when he starts moving."

"This is 2889 Lima—we'll be leaving 8,500 for 3,500.

"Roger, 89 Lima, advise heading," came the reply from the base.

"Will advise. 89 Lima."

The radar controller seemed a little confused, so I continued, "89 Lima is law enforcement aircraft—would appreciate your help."

"Roger, 89 Lima, understand."

From then on, we were cleared for any altitude or heading.

"The truck's moving," Lancaster and the ground radio reported at the same time. "We've got him," Lancaster answered.

"We're going to stand by in the dry dock area till you get him in a hole," a ground unit advised.

"Good idea," Lancaster answered.

We were on our own.

When the truck reached the city limits of Wilson, it pulled into a truck stop. We continued to circle the area. Ten minutes later the truck left, followed by a new white Pontiac. White cars are easy to spot from the air, but when we were trailing one it seemed that four out of five cars on the road were white.

"That Pontiac is definitely with the truck," Jim commented. "He passed it and hauled ass for about three miles. Now the truck has passed him and he's checking out the road behind the truck."

"Looks like he might be heading for the diggin's." This was a term I had picked up from Wally Hay, who had explained that back in the old gold rush days in Alaska the miners had to be very careful not to let anyone know where their mine, or diggings, was. When they went to the trading post for supplies they would take false trails and double back to make sure no one was following them. Moonshiners operated very much the same way when traveling to large illegal distilleries.

The truck headed south on Highway 58 to Kinston, then turned onto Highway 11 and continued south through an area that was almost completely devoid of humanity—remote to everything and everybody. The truck and Pontiac were the only two vehicles for eight miles in either direction.

"His lights just went out." Lancaster punched me on the shoulder.

I flipped off our navigation lights and slowly began a shallow turn. Both my navigation radios were set to VOR's (navigational radio beacons)—one to the north and the other to the east. I began twisting dials and centering the needles that would give me bearings from these stations to pinpoint my location.

"He's stopped, but the car is going on. Wait—the Pontiac just turned around and is headed back toward the truck," Jim reported.

I could see one set of lights, but couldn't pick out the truck. As the car slowed, the truck lights came on. The truck pulled back onto the pavement and turned into a driveway about a half-mile down the road.

When the truck began to move, I initiated a slow but steady climb. We soon reached 5,500 again.

"He's pulling into a big barn at the rear of the house." Lancaster's binoculars were trained on the truck, whose lights were doused again.

I kept my eye on the white Pontiac as it continued slowly back toward Kinston.

Making sure I had the correct coordinates for the barn on my nav radios, I swung the 172 back northwest toward Goldsboro.

"Meet us at the dock," Lancaster advised the ground units.

It was 11:00 P.M. when we reached the airport. We had been slow flying for four hours and I was beat.

Joe and the other agents were on top of the world when we told them the location of the barn and the actions of the convoy car.

"That's it," said Carter. "We'll be on the ground before daylight."

"We'll stand by here if you need the plane any more tonight."

I tilted the plane seat back and was asleep in ten minutes. At 2:30 A.M. someone banged on the plane door. It was Joe.

"We've got some movement. Can you get on it?"

"You bet," I said without thinking. As I began to taxi out to the end of the runway, I noticed that the sky was now overcast and some of the runway lights appeared a little fuzzy.

"Looks like a little weather has moved in," Jim commented. He was trying to tell me in a nice way that I should check the weather before taking off. I should have listened.

I poured the power to the 172, and one-third of the way down the runway I pulled the Cessna's nose up. Fifty feet into the air we hit solid soup.

"Oh, shit!" I muttered, quickly reducing the power and lowering the nose of the plane. The safe thing to do would have been to climb up through the overcast on instruments and go on to another airfield that was clear, but my first reaction was to get the nose back down and go back into Goldsboro. I might have to explain to the FAA why I made an instrument departure without a clearance. How stupid could I get? If I didn't make it back in, someone else would have to do the explaining—I would be dead.

But the good Lord was with me once again. We broke out of the clouds just as we passed over the end of the runway. I quickly added power, checked my airspeed and heading and reversed my course, staying beneath the low clouds.

As I lined up to land on the runway we had just departed, I was once again reminded that the 172 is a very forgiving airplane. If it were not, a lot of pilots would be pushing up daisies, myself included. When we got back on the ground, Lancaster said nothing. But he was ready to go again the next morning.

At ten o'clock the weather began to clear. We flew Carter over the suspected location and everyone agreed they could work it with ground units with the help of the radios I had brought.

I left in 2889 Lima at two that afternoon and arrived back in Atlanta four and one-half hours later—dog tired.

The North Carolina agents later made one of the largest seizures of an illicit distillery in eastern North Carolina, arresting four moonshiners in the process.

Perry Bloom, like J.R. Turner, eluded arrest once again.

Moonshiner loads liquor on back of truck in Jasper County, Georgia.

22.

SMOKEY BEAR

HEADQUARTERS CAME UP with another innovation in the late summer of 1969. This time it was a practical item being used by the military. Marvin Shaw called me in one morning and handed me a long black object that looked like a cross between a telescope and a long-lens camera.

"How about taking this up in the plane tonight and see if it would be of any help to you in the surveillance of ground objects," Shaw said. "Here's a book on how it works."

That afternoon Special Agent Wayne Wilson called from Jasper, Georgia. "Can you meet me at the Canton airport about midnight?" he asked.

"Ten-four. I've got some new equipment we need to try out anyway," I replied.

That night I met Dale Harbolt and Wally Hay at Gunn Airfield. Wally had absorbed the contents of the manual by that time and Dale and I took turns looking through the book. The principle behind the Starlite was that it magnified any light available by several hundred times, making it possible to see objects at night that could not be seen otherwise.

The military now has night-vision goggles that are descended from this first Starlite scope. It worked pretty well on the ground but we soon found that even though it had stabilizers built in, it was not very useful from the air.

At midnight Harbolt and I met Wilson at the Canton airport.

"We need to head north toward Jasper," Wayne said, throwing his gear into the back of 2889 Lima. "This guy is supposed to move after midnight. It should be a big outfit."

Nodding, I poured the power to the the 172 and we headed north.

"You can slow down now. He lives up here on the right."

No sooner had I pulled the power back than Wayne punched me.

"He's moving!"

It was 1:00 A.M. The pickup was moving north toward Talking Rock. Between Jasper and Talking Rock he turned right, crossed a railroad track and turned right again. The lights were extinguished and the truck moved another mile before turning in at a house with several chicken houses behind it.

"Okay, that's it," said Wayne.

Harbolt had been peering through the Starlite scope now for fifteen minutes.

"I'm about to get sick looking though this thing," he commented.

I had turned off my nav lights when the truck's lights went out. I began a slow easy turn back south.

"Can you find it on the ground?" I asked.

"I sure can. I know exactly where it is."

A week later Wayne called to say that they had seized a large still in one of the chicken houses and arrested three men. That was the kind of results I liked.

After that test flight we decided the scope would just be so much excess weight in the airplane, but it was encouraging to see the Treasury Department willing to spend money to equip its agents with advanced technology.

One morning Bill Griffin called the squad room.

"Charley, the State Bureau of Prisons just called. The state plane is out of service and they need some help. Eight prisoners escaped last night from a prison camp near Alto and four are still at large. All four are serving time for violent crimes so they want to apprehend them as soon as possible. Can you get a plane, go up there and fly out the area?"

"Yes, sir."

"Good. A couple of guards will meet you at the Cornelia Airport. What time will you be there?"

It was 11:00 A.M. "I'll be there at noontime," I replied.

It was late summer and the temperature was already in the high 80's when I poured the power to the 172. Airplanes fly better on cool days and as I lifted off the runway I could tell it was going to be a bumpy ride.

When I taxied up to the ramp at the small airport at Cornelia, two men walked toward the plane. One was dressed in green work clothes and the other had on a grey guard's uniform, complete with a Smokey Bear hat.

"You Charley Weems?" one of them asked.

"You got him. Are you ready to go?"

"We're ready," the uniformed guard replied emphatically.

Thinking that I'd better warn them of the bumpy ride we would be in for, I cautioned, "It's going to be a little rough out there this afternoon. If you start feeling bad, tell me. It's nothing to be ashamed of."

The one in green work clothes nodded his head.

The other one spoke up. "I was in the Air Force. Flying don't bother me," he boasted.

"All right, but let me know the minute you start feeling bad."

With that, we piled into the 172. Smokey Bear got in back. The guard up front directed me into the area of the search. I opened all the air vents and my side window. Several flights before, I had been making aerial photos and had removed a screw from a retainer bar on the window so that the window would be held up in flight by air pressure under the wing. It was wide open.

Looking down I could see men searching the area, some with bloodhounds and others with rifles. They meant business. The guard up front directed me where to fly. We were only about 300 feet off the ground, making steep turns first one way and then another. The outside air temperature gauge showed 90°F.

"Is everybody okay?" I asked casually.

"Yeah."

"Doing fine."

We continued to bounce in the turbulence and I kept my eye on the airport. Suddenly the man in front looked back.

"Are you okay?" he asked.

I knew what was happening, so I immediately turned toward the airport and applied full power.

"We'll be on the ground in five minutes," I tried to assure the back-seat passenger.

"It's a good thing you brought your hat," the man in green said.

Then it hit me—the unmistakable, indescribable odor of vomit. Nothing smells as bad, especially in a confined cabin of an airplane. I had closed my window when I increased speed to keep it from blowing off. It was probably a good thing. If that 140 mile per hour wind had been blowing into the back seat when the guard threw up, all of us would have been covered with vomit. He had filled his Smokey Bear hat.

As soon as we landed I piled out. Smokey took his hat to the bathroom and returned in a few minutes with some paper towels and a pan of soapy water. He had spilled a little climbing out, but soon cleaned it up—all but the smell, that is. I learned early to carry a spray can of Ozium. I soaked the soiled area with it and sprayed a generous amount all over the interior of the plane, then headed back to Atlanta.

The prisoners were finally rounded up that afternoon, but the old Air Force vet was not much good the rest of the day.

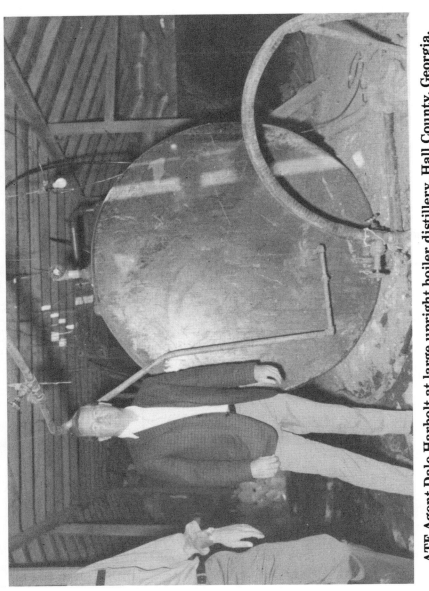

ATF Agent Dale Harbolt at large upright boiler distillery, Hall County, Georgia.

23.
MOON ROCKS

ON JULY 20, 1969, Neil Armstrong became the first man to set foot on the Moon. By December of 1972, twelve astronauts had explored the Moon and 843 pounds of moon rock had been brought back to the Houston Space Center for examination and testing. News of this rock filled the papers.

In September of 1969, ATF Agent Wally Williams, one of the many characters in ATF, came up with some small authentic looking pieces of moon rock. I was privileged to see these objects of antiquity at the little Canton, Georgia airport. Williams had called from his post of duty at Rome requesting air support in trailing a major violator in Cherokee County.

When Dale Harbolt and I landed at Canton, Williams was waiting for us. After some preliminary small talk, Wally called me aside. Looking around to make sure no one was nearby, he asked confidentially, "Have you seen my moon rocks?"

"She-it," I said, grinning.

Wally looked hurt. "No, really—I've got a good friend who works at the Houston Space Center. I've been begging him ever since the astronauts got back to send me a piece of moon rock. He finally did, but not without swearing me to secrecy as to where I got it."

With that, Wally opened the trunk of the government car. He looked around furtively once more, then reached in, pulled out a small cardboard box and handed it to me.

Knowing Williams had a reputation for playing jokes, sometimes sophisticated ones requiring weeks of preparation, I took the box gingerly. I examined it closely, looking at the address, the return address which said "Houston Space Center," the postmark which seemed authentic, and began to wonder if it indeed was a joke. Still not convinced, I carefully opened the box. Inside was another box filled with cotton. There was a letter folded on top of the cotton.

Wally held the box carefully while I opened the sheet of paper. The official-looking letter began, "Dear Wally." It explained how this friend of Wally's would be in very deep trouble if anyone ever found out he had sent these pieces of history to him. The friend went on to say that he owed Wally a favor and that this would cancel all obligations, and concluded by saying that Wally should protect the pieces of moon rock at all costs. It was very impressive, indeed.

Now came the big moment. I was going to see pieces of the Moon close up and maybe even get to hold them.

Carefully, Wally removed the cotton from the box. In the bottom, resting on some more cotton, were the moon rocks. I looked closely. They appeared very similar to stove clinkers I remembered from my childhood that resulted from burning low grade coal containing a lot of iron.

Not wanting to hurt Wally's feelings again, I continued to examine carefully the contents of the box. These clinkers had faint shades of blue and pink color in places. I wondered how that could be.

"What do you think?" Wally asked.

"I don't know," I said evasively. "Looks like clinkers to me."

"You've never seen clinkers with blue and red in them, have you?" Wally was growing defensive.

"Naw, I guess not." I handed the secret box back to him. "Let's go to work."

Wally grinned and put the box back into the trunk.

Sometime later I heard a story from several different sources and Wally did not deny it.

One afternoon Williams showed his moon rocks to a north Georgia sheriff. The sheriff was impressed. Wally played it cool, but the next week he just happened by the sheriff's office again.

"Do you have those moon rocks with you?" was the first thing the sheriff asked.

"Yeah, I think they're in the car," Wally answered casually.

"Can I see them again?" The sheriff was eager.

Wally brought the clinkers in.

"Boy, I sure would like to have a piece of one of those," the sheriff said, looking longingly at the items in the small box. "Couldn't you let me have just a small piece? I'll trade you or buy one from you!"

"Naw, I couldn't sell it, that wouldn't be right," Wally pondered.

The sheriff had a small lamp that was handmade from a copper still he had seized years before. The lamp was in the shape of a miniature still and Wally had always coveted it.

"If you won't tell anyone, I'll try to break off a small chunk but this moon rock is awfully hard. Would you trade me that moonshine still lamp for a piece of my rock?" Wally leaned close to the sheriff's ear, playing him like a big fish on the line.

"I don't know—I think a lot of that lamp."

"Okay, then." Wally turned to go.

"Wait, wait—I'll do it. I've got to have a piece of the Moon." The sheriff gave in.

Wally carefully removed a piece of clinker from the box. When he couldn't break off a piece with his hands, the sheriff handed him a pair of pliers.

Carefully Wally pinched the end of the object. "I don't want to crush it."

When a small piece finally broke off Wally was quick to brush the piece and all the fragments into an envelope furnished by the sheriff.

"Wally, I'll never forget you for this," the sheriff said happily as Wally left with the lamp. The sheriff immediately put the envelope containing his moon rock into a safety deposit box at the bank.

Some weeks later when the story of Wally's moon rock hoax began to get around, the sheriff found out he had been taken. He didn't like it, but being a good sport he decided to get even.

One day Frank Sells, an FBI agent who had worked the northeast Georgia area for some time, walked into the sheriff's office. "Frank, I want you to help me with something," the sheriff said.

He told Frank how he had been tricked by Williams.

"What can I do?" asked Frank.

"Just go along—I'm going to get the U.S. Attorney, a friend of mine, to tell Wally very confidentially that you are investigating Wally for using the U.S. Mail to defraud—that you know about the so-called moon rocks from Houston and intend to get to the bottom of it. The U.S. Attorney will also tell Wally that he had better get this thing straightened out before his ATF supervisors hear about it."

"All right, I'll go along with you," Frank agreed. "Knowing Wally, he'll probably contact me personally as soon as he hears this."

Two days later Frank's telephone rang. "Frank, this is Wally Williams in Rome. I need to talk to you."

"Sure, Wally. How about meeting me at Riggelo's Restaurant in Rome at seven tomorrow night. Oh, and by the way, bring that copper lamp with you."

Wally was stunned. Now he was sure the FBI was on his case. He worried all the next day.

Frank called the sheriff and told him the plan. "Come to Riggelo's at twenty after seven tonight if you want a free meal off Wally. Bring as many people as you like. We'll be in the back."

Frank made Wally sweat blood for 20 minutes, then agreed to drop the so-called investigation if Wally would return the lamp to the sheriff and buy everyone's dinner that night. Wally's practical joke cost him more than $100.

The sheriff had the last laugh after all.

★ ★ ★

1969 was winding down and it was rumored that the region was going to set up an air operations program and assign several agents to be full time special agent/pilots working out of the regional office. That sounded like a dream come true for me.

I talked to Marvin Shaw.

"All right, Charley, but you'll have to request reassignment to the regional office. You'll be the first full-time pilot. You realize that your advancement potential will be limited if you give up the Area Supervisor job?"

"That's okay," I quickly answered. "I don't want to miss out on flying full time."

I requested reassignment in writing and reported back to the regional office on September 7. My forays into other states would certainly pick up now.

The first week, I was called to North Carolina and Alabama to assist with the airplane in the surveillance of distilleries and shipments of moonshine, in addition to working with Bob Scott in Gainesville and Leon Estep in Cornelia. There was always plenty to do.

On my birthday, September 23, Leon Estep and I took off from Gainesville airport.

"This guy is supposed to move just after dark," Leon said.

The sun was fading as 2889 Lima purred in the evening air. What better way to spend your birthday!

The ATF radio crackled. "He's loading up." It was Hugh Merrill.

Estep began to scan the Cornelia area. "The warehouse is just ahead."

I flipped off the navigation lights and throttled back.

"I see the truck," Estep reported to Merrill. "We've got him."

For the next ten minutes we circled the area, very high and very slow.

"He's moving!" Merrill whispered. Observing criminal activity is always a high wire act. We had to get in close enough to see what was going on, yet be careful not to be seen and blow the whole operation.

The truck turned north on U.S. 441. As it passed through Clarkesville, it slowed. A dark blue Pontiac wheeled past, blinked his lights and continued north. The truck followed.

"I'll keep an eye on the car. You watch the truck," I told Estep.

Five miles north of Clarkesville the car suddenly whipped into an abandoned service station and headed back south. The truck continued past the station.

"We must be close," Leon commented.

The Pontiac made a U-turn in the highway and headed north again, passing the truck at a high rate of speed. The truck turned off the highway onto a small dirt road and cut its lights.

"Did he stop?" I asked.

"No, he's driving without lights." Estep's eyes were glued on the truck.

I began tuning the aircraft navigation radios to pinpoint the location.

"He just pulled in past a small house. There's two big chicken houses behind it."

Easing the 172 into a shallow bank, I began a turn back toward Cornelia. We both agreed that had to be the still location.

At 10:30 I pulled the nose of the 172 back into the evening sky after dropping Estep off at the Gainesville airport. The trip back to Gunn Airfield was one of the most pleasant of my career. It was a smooth fall night with a full Moon. People who feel that they are very important and that the world can't do without them should fly alone some clear, starry night and look around. On a clear night you can see for miles. The lights of little towns and big cities dot the ground below. In vast rural areas, security lights are scattered here and there. I thought, Here I am 10,000 feet above all these people, some asleep, some at work. They all have their troubles, joys and frustrations. They don't even know I exist. How important does that make me? Not very. If I were to suddenly disappear from the face of the earth, my family and friends—maybe two dozen people—would miss me for a short time. Any self-important attitude one might have quickly fades away high in the night sky—especially when alone.

Three nights later, I was flying with Agent Don Jones in the Athens and Commerce areas. We heard Leon Estep on the radio.

"This is 670. Did you do any good on that thing we worked the other night?"

"Ten-four. We're on it now," Estep replied.

I felt good again.

Sometime later, agents working the Tallapoosa, Georgia area located a distillery in the small abandoned St. Budapest Catholic Church near Tallapoosa. Jim Elder, being Catholic, took a lot of good-natured kidding over that one. You didn't have to have a thick skin to work for ATF, but it helped.

CHARLES WEEMS EXAMINES FELT HAT USED AS STRAINER
Federal Officers Found Chicken House Used for Still

24.

WELL-OILED MACHINE

SINCE THE SEIZURE of the big outfit in Heard County we had been too busy to devote much time to Arvin Carter. We figured by now he must be feeling neglected. One day after Dale Harbolt and I flew 2889 Lima for four hours straight in Douglas and south Fulton County trailing Carter, we landed at the Fulton County airport and topped off the tanks. Dale came back into the terminal where I was checking weather.

"Charley, Koppe just called. They've got a truck headed south driven by Willie Jarboe. They need help trailing him."

"Okay, let's go."

We received another immediate clearance from Fulton County tower and turned south.

"Atlanta Approach, this is 2889 Lima, just off Fulton County, climbing to two point five. Looks like we'll be in your traffic area shortly. Would appreciate any help you can give us."

One of the controllers who had worked me a number of times through the dense air traffic answered.

"Roger, 89 Lima. Maintain 2,000 for now. Say intentions."

"Eight-nine Lima will be working with a ground unit on the South Expressway, probably heading south."

"Roger, 89 Lima, maintain two."

Harbolt had been talking to Koppe on the other radio. "He's at University Avenue headed south."

"Atlanta Approach, 89 Lima at 2,000. We can go lower if necessary."

"Roger, 89 Lima, descend and maintain 1,800. That will keep you under the departing traffic."

"Roger."

"I have the truck. He's almost to the Ford Plant," Harbolt reported to Koppe.

"Good. We'll fall back." Koppe sounded relieved.

Slowing down, we had little trouble following the small van truck. It was getting dark, and there was a running light with the yellow lens broken on the top right hand side of the van. It shone bright white and made the truck easy to spot.

The truck continued south into Henry County. Near McDonough when he turned back west, we knew we were getting close.

"Hold up in McDonough," Harbolt radioed to Koppe.

We had been working together using the plane for about four years now, and could anticipate each other's actions much the way ballplayers do after playing together for years. It had to be a team effort with the air and ground units working together.

When the truck cut his lights and pulled to the rear of a remote farmhouse, I said, "We'll just bide our time."

Thirty minutes later Harbolt punched me on the shoulder. "He's leaving."

I had been deep in thought—almost asleep—flying the 172 in smooth circles.

Koppe was waiting at the highway back to Atlanta. As soon as they had the truck in sight, I headed for Gunn Airfield. On the way home that night Koppe called and said they had seized the truck on I-285 near Campbellton Road and arrested Jarboe with 288 gallons of moonshine.

The next day I flew over the farm house and could see vehicle sign leaving the back yard and disappearing into the woods. I figured the still had to be there. Three days later Chuck Lowe and Hiram Cook made two arrests and destroyed the 2,000 gallon ground hog still.

Being available at a moment's notice and being able to make on-the-spot decisions without fear of second-guessing paid off.

Most of October and November I spent in south Georgia working with Vic Bernhardt and Leon Estep on major violator Jake Brady in Vidalia, Lyons, Swainsboro, McRae, Eastman and Dublin.

Our work finally paid off the first week in December when we trailed a load of sugar to a large distillery in the vicinity of Louisville, Georgia. Vic secured enough evidence to make a good conspiracy case against Charlie Joe Vess, one of the largest operators in south Georgia.

★ ★ ★

Just when you think you have seen it all, something happens in a most unusual way.

Jim Elder and I had been sitting at Gunn Airfield all night long waiting for a radio call from Koppe. He had a liquor car under surveillance and the information was that the car would leave the Atlanta area around midnight, pick up a load of moonshine and return about seven the next morning, blending in with the morning work traffic coming into Atlanta.

At 5:30 A.M. the radio crackled. "670, we might as well knock off and try him again tomorrow night." It was Koppe.

"Ten-four," Elder responded.

I started up the government car. We hit I-20 and headed west towards Atlanta. Elder spoke up.

"I'm hungry. Let's stop here at the Waffle Hut and check it out."

"Sounds good to me."

Even though it was early morning the parking lot was full of cars and pickup trucks. As we stood in the door I could see that it was a popular place. A counter with stools ran the length of the small building and only a narrow walkway separated the customers from the grill, cabinets and built-in refrigerator. A short, red-haired cook was throwing frozen potatoes and bacon strips onto the grill, frying eggs and operating a four-slot toaster at the same time. A waitress in her late thirties, who had seen better days, brushed her hair back as she scurried around taking care of the six small booths on the opposite wall.

"There's two leaving the counter. Let's get those seats." We worked our way past the two construction workers and sat down at the counter, directly across from the grill.

Without asking, the waitress set two steaming cups of coffee before us, scribbled down our order and was gone. As we sat eating our scrambled eggs and bacon, I was amazed at the efficiency of the harried and overworked cook. He moved like a well-oiled machine.

Jim and I were just finishing our breakfast when a man wearing a Texaco uniform arrived, sat down next to Jim and ordered two eggs over light with hash browns. Suddenly the cook headed for the storeroom in the back. He returned quickly with a package of frozen hash browns and threw them into the refrigerator next to the grill. He turned back to the grill to check the food.

"BLUACHHHHHH—"

I couldn't believe my eyes. The cook was throwing up right on the hot grill. As the vomit began to sizzle and steam, the bedraggled waitress turned to me.

"That last drink must have got to him." With that, she turned and walked away. The cook went back into the storeroom.

The vomit continued to fry. Shortly, the cook returned, took a spatula and began to scrape the mess into a slot at the rear of the grill. He poured cooking oil onto the grill along with two handfuls of frozen hash browns, spreading them liberally over the cooking surface. After some thirty seconds he scraped them into the slot and took up where he left off, cooking potatoes, bacon and eggs on the grill. Elder and I looked at each other in amazement.

The well-oiled cook slid the Texaco man's eggs onto a plate with the hash browns and commented, "I busted the yellow on one of your eggs."

"That's all right," replied the man wearing the star, and dug in.

He must have been awfully hungry.

25.

WEATHER WOES

FLYING ON INSTRUMENTS in solid instrument conditions requires complete concentration. I had received my instrument "ticket" about a year before but had accrued very little actual time in the clouds. Flying alone in these conditions at night is even more tedious.

One day in the middle of June, Regional Special Ed Gray called from Raleigh, N.C. "Charley, can you fly up and bring us three of those portable radios you've been using in the airplane? We're in a bind and need them by tonight. I've checked the weather and it should be okay except for a few thunderstorms."

"I'll be at the old Raleigh airport at four-thirty. If I can't get there I'll call your office."

"Ten-four."

I checked with the Flight Service Station in Atlanta and found that the weather was supposed to hold until about eight o'clock. After eight they were forecasting low stratus clouds with a possibility of thundershowers up until daybreak.

I can make it to Raleigh. If it looks too bad later on, I'll just spend the night and come back tomorrow in good weather, I reasoned.

As usually happens when you're pushed for time, the telephone rang. After two lengthy phone conversations, and replacing the batteries in one of the radios, I finally left Atlanta in 2889 Lima at 1:00 P.M. By the time I reached the Georgia-South Carolina line I could tell this was not going to be easy. I ran into a line of thunderstorms south of Greenville and was forced to land at Anderson.

An hour later, the weather cleared. I took off for Raleigh. Although I was two hours late, Ed Gray and Joe Carter were waiting for me. We quickly unloaded the radios and I checked again with the FAA for the weather forecast. It was the same as before, only worse.

"I've got to get going if I'm going to get back into Atlanta tonight," I told the two agents.

"Well, come on and eat supper with us before you go. I know you're hungry," insisted Carter.

He was right—I was hungry. An hour later I called the FAA again. "Low stratus formations with indefinite ceilings vicinity Fayetteville, N.C. and Augusta, Georgia. Raleigh 2,000 broken going to 500 overcast by midnight. Not recommended for VFR (visual flight)."

"Looks like I'm going to have to stay here. How about taking me to a motel?" I asked Ed.

"The furniture people are in town for a convention and there's not a room available," grinned Joe. "You can stay at my apartment tonight. I've got an extra bed."

"You're sure it won't put you out?"

"Naw—I might have some female company later but if I do, I'll get her to bring a friend."

My mind was racing. I had heard some of the stories going around the region about Joe Carter's wild parties and I was sure I didn't want to get involved in one that night. Besides, I was dead tired.

"Let me check weather again," I said, heading for the phone.

This was the same drill that I have read about in aircraft accident reports time after time. The pilot, away from home, keeps calling the weather people hoping for a better forecast. When he gets none, he takes off anyway, saying to himself that he can always turn back, but he doesn't and winds up another statistic. It's called "get home-itis!" and I had a bad case.

"Ed, if you'll take me back to the airport, I think I can make it back to Atlanta by staying under this stuff."

"Whatever you say, Charley."

As I took off from Raleigh that night I knew I was not using good judgment. By now the clouds were solid overcast at 2,000 feet. As I headed south the ceiling became lower. Navigating off VOR radio stations in the area, I began to lose the signals about 40 miles south of Raleigh. Fumbling for new maps and different radio frequencies for other VOR stations, I found myself flying lower and lower to stay under the clouds. When I lost both navigational radio signals, I decided to call Fayetteville Approach Control Radar.

"Fayetteville approach, this is 2889 Lima about 20 southwest of Fayetteville."

"Roger, 89 Lima, squawk 5343."

I switched my transponder to 5343 and looked up to see myself engulfed in clouds. I pushed the nose over gently and in a few seconds emerged from the clouds, but only about 800 feet above the ground.

"89 Lima squawking 5343," I called to Fayetteville, hoping against hope they could pick me up on radar.

"No contact, 89 Lima. You're probably too low for us to pick you up."

"Roger, Fayetteville. Could I get an IFR clearance to climb up through this stuff and get on top to continue to Atlanta?" I asked hopefully.

"Negative, 89 Lima. Cannot give you a clearance until I have you positively identified. Do you want to declare an emergency?"

"Negative. Eight-nine Lima." My pride and the thought of all the explanations and reports I would have to make to the FAA if I declared an emergency overwhelmed my common sense. I plunged on through the dark, foggy night. Fatigue had dulled my senses and I was on the verge of becoming one of those accident statistics.

By now I was down to 600 feet and could see absolutely no lights anywhere on the ground. I found out later I was over the Pee Dee Wildlife Reservation.

I tuned radios to different frequencies with one hand and tried to hold a sectional map and the wheel with the other, glancing up occasionally.

Suddenly, something told me to look out the side window and down. There was the most beautiful sight I had ever seen—runway lights—a simple runway in the middle of nowhere. I had no idea where I was.

I pulled the power back on the 172, laid it on its side and lined up with the lights. The sound of those tires squealing on the asphalt runway was beautiful.

It was totally pitch dark in all directions. As I taxied up to a small building and cut my landing light and engine, there was nothing but total silence. For a few seconds I wondered if I was dreaming. Then I thanked the good Lord for bringing me out of another predicament. If I hadn't looked out of that window at the precise second I did, I wouldn't have seen the runway. I certainly could have wound up hitting a tall tower or a hill somewhere down the line. It was truly a miracle.

After my brief prayer of thanks, I climbed out and tried to figure out where I was. Automobile headlights suddenly lit up the airplane. As I walked toward the car, my pride left me. My first words to the two teenagers were, "Where am I?"

They had seen my landing light and were curious. I guess they were expecting a crash.

"You're in Pageland, South Carolina."

I had never heard of Pageland and had not seen any lights of a town before I landed.

"Pageland is about three miles from here," one of the young men volunteered.

"Is there a telephone anywhere near here?"

"No, the closest one is in town. We'll drive you in if you want to go."

"Okay, but I want to pay you because I'll need you to bring me back after I make the phone call."

I called the FAA and told them I had landed safely in Pageland so they wouldn't be searching for me the next day. I spent the night in the back seat of 2889 Lima.

The next morning the weather continued to be rotten but about ten o'clock it cleared enough for me to take off. This time I got as far as Winnsboro, South Carolina before low ceilings forced me down. I knew where I was, though, and contacted the Columbia Post of Duty on the ATF frequency. I advised them I was landing at Winnsboro Airport.

Any old port in a storm, I figured. From the air I could tell the grass strip didn't get much use. I flared out over the runway and touched down. High grass hit the metal fuselage. I held it off and landed 100 feet further down, running through a large mud puddle. I finally got the plane stopped near an old, ramshackle building. I got out to look around, then pushed the plane to one side though it really wasn't necessary. It looked as if no one had landed here in over a year.

An hour later the ATF radio came to life. It was Special Agent Hudson Waller.

"Six-seventy, I'll be there in about 15. I've had a hard time finding you."

"Ten-four."

Hudson pulled into what had once been the drive-way to the airstrip, a big grin on his face. "I didn't even know this place was here, and I work this territory! I stopped at the sheriff's office and asked how to get to the Winnsboro Airport. They said there wasn't one. When I persisted, someone finally remembered there had been one here about three years ago but it had been closed since that time. How'd you find it?"

"It's a long story."

We drove into Columbia and I had lunch with SAC Louis Fisher and ASAC Dave Edmisten. By 2:30 P.M. the weather had cleared enough for me to fly back to Atlanta. I was glad to get home!

★ ★ ★

The following Friday I received a call from ATF Agent Riley Oxley in Albany, Georgia.

"Charley, a lot of automatic weapons have been disappearing from the Naval Air Station near here. After extensive observations and undercover work we've come up with a prime suspect for the thefts. It's a civilian who works at the air station. He's supposed to deliver several fully automatic weapons to one of our undercover agents tonight. We'd like to trail him after he gets off work and find out where the weapons are hidden."

"Sounds good. I'll be there this afternoon."

I called and got approval to land at the military base in the Cessna 172. Jim Elder went along with me as observer. When I contacted the control tower that afternoon and advised I would be landing at the base, there appeared to be some confusion.

"Stand by, 2889 Lima. Do you have prior approval to land?"

"Roger. U.S. Treasury Department aircraft. Check with Captain Smythe."

In 1969, in the midst of the Viet Nam conflict, the Naval Air Station at Albany was home base for some of the most sophisticated aircraft in the world. Here I was in a Cessna 172 with 150 horsepower, 140 miles per hour top speed, mixing in with fighters and reconnaissance jets capable of flying more than 1,500 m.p.h.

"Two-eight-eight-niner Lima is cleared to land on Runway two-niner. Report gear down and locked."

This was standard procedure for the military tower personnel, to make sure the gear was lowered.

I answered, "Roger, 89 Lima cleared to land two-nine. Gear down and welded." No response from the tower to my little joke.

Lining up on final, I was all set to touch down on the end of the runway.

"Eight-niner Lima, caution. Restraining cable 600 feet from end of runway."

About that time, I saw it. A one-inch steel cable was strung across the runway for use by Navy jets to practice carrier landings, catching the cable on their tailhooks. If I had hit that thing with the wheels of the little 172, they would have had to carry it off in a basket. I passed barely three feet over the cable and muttered into the microphone, "I appreciate that."

"I'm just glad he said something." Elder had a point.

That night, we took off just before dusk and trailed the suspect to a wooded area adjacent to the Marine Supply Depot. After we had been watching him for two hours, lightning began growing in intensity in the west. I maintained constant communication with the air station control tower because we were working over the end of the 12,000 foot runway.

"Two-eight-eight-niner Lima, there's a squall line of severe thunderstorms just west of here. Will be in our area in ten minutes. Thought you'd like to know."

Just then, a McDonnell F-4 Phantom flashed by our left wing in a steep turn toward the air base. The F-4 weighed more than 54,000 pounds. If he thinks it's time to set down, I know I do, I mused.

"Tell the ground units we're going in."

Elder reached for the ATF radio. At the same time I was on the aircraft radio to the tower.

"Albany, this is 89 Lima. Request landing instructions."

"Roger, eight-niner Lima, follow the F-4 turning final for two-niner."

"Roger. How about landing on the taxiway. I don't think this weather will wait."

There was a pause, then, "Eight-niner Lima cleared to land on Runway two-niner taxiway. Clear as soon as possible."

"Eight-nine Lima. Yes, sir!" I rolled the Cessna over and peeled off to the left.

Elder climbed up front with me to help watch for the F-4. "He's on final," Jim reported.

I dropped full flaps and pulled the throttle all the way back. We descended at a steep angle.

"I'm going to try to get on the ground and out of his way before the storm hits." By now the wind was gusting severely. I leveled out about ten feet above the taxiway, let the airspeed bleed off and set the plane down.

I had no sooner touched the tarmac than the storm hit. Rain came down in sheets and the wind was gusting so hard that it took full power to move forward. Four sailors came running out to the Cessna, motioning me to the right. Two grabbed a wing strut on each side.

"Jim, get out and help them hold this thing until they can get it tied down," I shouted over the wind.

I have never seen a heavier rain. The wind was almost lifting the 172 off the pavement. I kept the engine revved up in order to stay in one spot. Finally, the sailors attached lines to the Cessna and I was able to shut it down. Jim and I made a dash for the briefing room. We were soaked to the skin but thankful to be on the ground.

Even though we had to pull the plane off the suspect, we trailed him long enough for the ground units to get the evidence they needed for the prosecution of this individual and the recovery of eight M-16's.

Another unforgettable night.

26.
DAZZLE 'EM WITH PAPERWORK

THE KEY TO success in government agencies is not necessarily the *quantity* of results you get—it's how well you can turn failure *into* success by use of the written word. I have seen it done time after time.

The first week in November, Wally Hay walked into the regional squad room. Calling me aside, he began to tell me about a project he had been working on for several months—another Top Secret attempt to locate moonshine distilleries using the very latest scientific methods. He had been working with a big defense contractor in Texas and had persuaded the powers-that-be that this would be a feasible solution to finding a large number of stills in a short time, applying military techniques for our purposes.

As special agents with ATF, we all had received Top Secret clearances, but gaining access to some of the techniques and equipment used by the military required that we be cleared further on a need-to-know basis. Wally worked it all out, and used his tremendous persuasive powers to secure $30,000 from the Regional Commissioner of Internal Revenue to test his theories. That in itself was no small feat.

Wally briefed me on the area we would be covering and asked me to secure necessary county maps and try to locate several active stills north and east of Dawsonville and Dahlonega. I had spent the better part of three years working in the test area. All that week, Hugh Merrill and I worked to locate several stills, not knowing what we were going to do with them.

On the night of November 13 I met Wally and the pilots and technicians from Texas at Peachtree-DeKalb Airport. Wally led me over to an old DC-3. As I climbed on board, it brought back old memories of my first airplane ride, in a C-47, the military version of a DC-3. Instead of landing with the plane, I had jumped out at 2,000 feet over Fort Benning, Georgia during my paratrooper training.

A number of cameras were mounted in the floor of the old airplane. There was a large black box affair with cables and wires running to other black boxes.

"That's the detector system. I'll explain how it works later," Wally commented casually.

The old radial engines coughed, black smoke belched from the exhausts and the vibration and feel of power took over.

Wally went forward and I followed after the take-off. We watched the pilots check coordinates and maps and at 1:00 A.M. we began our first run over the target area.

We flew at exactly 2,000 feet above the terrain in a straight line for about 20 miles. The operator of the black box was monitoring our progress. A high-pitched humming noise emanated from another box.

"What's that?" I asked.

"The cryogenic cooler," Wally quickly cut me off.

I must have asked something I shouldn't, so I turned my attention back to the cockpit. We were getting very close to the high mountains that flank Dahlonega on the north and east. The pilots had apparently set their navigational radios to certain radials in degrees from the station. When the radio needle swung to center, they would turn to a new heading. The closer we got to the mountains, the more the co-pilot tapped the nav needle with his finger, hoping to make it move. He readjusted it several times.

"This thing can't be right," he muttered to the pilot. Just then it swung around. As the old workhorse airplane began a steep turn to the right, there was an audible sigh of relief. We continued back south in a straight line and repeated the procedure six times, then headed back to Atlanta.

Hay had made arrangements for the processing of the film at Dobbins Air Force Base. At five that morning we received the film back in negative form and rushed it to the Federal Building where we excitedly began scanning it with small magnifying glasses. Features on the terrain showed up amazingly well on the negatives. We could match up roads with those on the county maps and also see outlines of streams and buildings. The hotter the object, the brighter the image on the film.

The theory was that a moonshine distillery would produce heat whether in operation or not. The heat source used to produce the whiskey would certainly show up on the film. If not in operation, the ferment ing mash would produce heat which would also show up. The flights were made after midnight to allow much of the radiated heat in the terrain to dissipate. Winter would be the best time to do this because of the greater contrast in temperatures.

Wally Hay explained it all later as follows:

"We are initiating an undertaking to ascertain the theoretic and technical parameters as well as study the potential application of using military type infrared sensor systems to pinpoint the location of illicit distilleries in the southeastern United States. We will initiate an instructional and consultive review of the nature and capability of I.R. systems integrated with the characteristics of illicit distilleries. We are operating under the assumption that certain thermal and emissive characteristics are inherent in illicit distillery operations. The probability exists that the detection of illicit distilleries by airborne infrared scanning is feasible." It *sounded* good, anyway.

"Here's one," Wally's voice filled the room. Everyone rushed to Wally's side. He pointed to a bright white spot, apparently deep in the woods off a small county road north of Cumming. The location was certainly in still country and I could think of no other reason for a source of heat in a place like that.

"It's got to be," I agreed.

We soon spotted another intense source of heat at the rear of a large building behind a house.

"I'll bet that's where they're dumping their spent mash from a still in the barn," I concluded quickly. Everyone agreed.

We found several more suspect locations and then went home around noontime to get some rest, 30 hours after we had started. I went to sleep with visions of seizing J.R. Turner's distillery in a matter of days using this new, revolutionary method. I could hardly wait.

That night we met again at the PDK Airport and made plans for a second flight. Flying northeast of Atlanta in the Winder-Athens area, we repeated the procedure. After another 16 hour day we made plans to fly to Dallas, Texas with the crew in the DC-3. I was pleased to be let in on the initial phase of the operation. This was big! Or as Barney Fife would say, "really big!"

The weather was bad on Saturday night so the flight was postponed until Monday. I was glad to get some rest and let all the big-time technical jargon sink into my overloaded brain.

Monday morning we took off for Dallas in the DC-3 and arrived nine hours later, after a slow and bumpy ride. We headed immediately to the company's facilities, where with more experts we looked at the film again.

We finally quit at midnight and once again, I had no trouble getting to sleep. Wally and I spent four days going through the giant complex where the detector and hundreds of other highly sensitive devices were manufactured for the military and other government agencies, including the C.I.A. People in white gowns, caps and masks worked in sterile glass-enclosed rooms. The place was cleaner than any hospital I've ever been in. It was an interesting and informative tour.

Friday night we flew back to Atlanta, worn out but excited at the prospect of checking out our finds.

The following Monday, I contacted ATF agents in Gainesville and Athens and gave them the locations of possible distillery sites in their areas. I saved the two sites Wally and I had first spotted that looked too good to be true.

The next day it was cold and cloudy. I called the Gainesville office. My old friend Hugh Merrill answered.

"What are you doing?" I asked.

"I'm down here for federal court but my case got put off. You need any help?"

"Sure do—how about meeting me at the courthouse in Cumming in an hour. You got any work clothes?"

"Got 'em in my car. See you in Cumming."

Driving north out of Atlanta, I remembered one of my first undercover assignments in the Cumming area with Red Martin, one of many ATF agents killed in the line of duty. Hugh was waiting when I arrived. I grabbed my portable radio and got into the car with him.

"Just head north toward Coal Mountain. I want you to drop me out on the first road south of there. Give me an hour and come back through. If I'm not there, give me another hour."

We turned right on the secondary road into an area that had once been densely wooded but which now was stripped of most of its trees by logging.

"Good place for a still," Hugh mused.

"I hope so."

Hugh dropped me off and I made my way slowly parallel to the public road until I found the old woods road I was looking for. Not much travel sign on it, I thought. I became more cautious the further I walked into the sparsely wooded area. Around a bend in the road I was suddenly confronted with a huge sawdust pile. A sawmill had once stood in this location but had been moved out. The sawdust pile was all that was left. I searched the area but could find no other sign of travel away from there. This had to be the right place.

It was a cold morning and I began to wonder if the sawdust would be warmer than the outside air. I pushed my bare hand deep into the pile and found the answer. It was very warm—almost hot—inside. Fermentation, the process vegetation goes through when rotting, was taking place in the organic matter of the sawdust. Lesson Number One: Don't jump to conclusions.

A later check of the area with a thermometer showed the outside air temperature to be 48°F, the ground 44° and the interior of the sawdust pile, 78°.

I made my way back to the dropoff point, where Hugh picked me up.

"There was nothing to the information, but I've got another place I want to look at, north of Coal Mountain. Maybe this will turn out to be something."

As agents we all received some good information, some bad and a lot in between. Hugh understood.

As we passed the farmhouse I had seen on the film, I peered at it intently. It was in plain view from the highway and in the rear was a large fenced-in lot where dairy cows were penned before milking. The lot was covered with cow manure. Well, now we know cow manure gives off heat, I thought. We certainly won't have any trouble finding cow lots or sawdust piles. This technique was not going to be the all-purpose answer I had thought in the beginning.

Although few positive results were achieved from the initial flight, Wally was not discouraged. He plunged into the effort even harder than before, determined to prove that we could find stills using infrared sensing devices.

A good example of "dazzling 'em with paperwork" took place in the seventies when federal law enforcement agencies began to concentrate heavily on organized crime. Several ATF agents were assigned to the Organized Crime Task Force in Miami. About two years after its inception I attended an explosives school at Fort Gordon, Georgia and talked to an agent who had been on the task force for over a year. He was expounding on how well they were doing and on the great success the task force was having in Miami.

"How many people have you arrested?" was my first question.

He looked amazed. "What do you mean?"

"Just what I said. How many people has the task force put in jail?"

"We're an intelligence-gathering agency," he stammered defensively. "We've gathered a tremendous amount of intelligence on these individuals."

"What good does all the intelligence in the world do if you don't put a stop to violations of the law by prosecuting people?"

"You don't understand," he explained patiently. "We just gather information."

Knowing there was no need to argue, I let it drop. As a law enforcement officer, I felt my job was to gather evidence, make arrests and protect the country from the criminal element. It was that simple.

I continued to check out infrared sensing information when Wally requested it, but I soon lost enthusiasm for these highly technical methods. I went on my way trailing violators with the airplane and finding stills the old fashioned way.

Special Agent Bill Ivey from the Tuscaloosa, Alabama office and Agent Maxwell Duke from the Macon office were working full time on the project, so it gave me the freedom to do what I enjoyed the most.

While I was flying almost every day trailing vehicles and locating stills, Wally was working long and hard on the infrared program. He had received approval and more money to pursue the idea that we could find illegal distilleries economically using this technique. Duke and Ivey assisted Hay in collecting technical data and in writing the reams of paperwork justifying the time and money expended in the operation.

Infrared surveillance flights were taking place in Georgia, Alabama, Mississippi and North Carolina. The film would be studied by Hay, Ivey and Duke and suspicious hot spots pinpointed. The locations were furnished to the agents working that particular area. About one in ten proved to be a moonshine still, but the technique was still in an experimental stage.

The last week in August, about two o'clock one morning the twin engine plane flown by pilots of the Houston military contractor made its approach to land in Mobile, Alabama. It was following a DC-9 and the night was clear and the wind calm. Suddenly the plane rolled left violently and before the pilot could correct, the aircraft hit the ground. All on board except the copilot were killed. ATF Special Agent Jim Patterson was one of the fatalities. He was flying with the infrared operators, pointing out areas to be covered for the survey. Thus ATF lost another fine young man in the line of duty. It was a tragic loss and would have doomed the infrared project if it hadn't been for Wally's determination and persistence.

One of the military's infrared scanners was lost in the crash also, but through Wally's persuasion another was secured and the survey continued.

(It was determined that wake turbulence from the preceding DC-9 was probably the cause of the crash.)

Meanwhile, I continued working independently with a leased 172 all over the southeast where needed, on one occasion assisting the FBI in a search near Columbus, Georgia for a bank robber. It was good to feel needed, especially by the FBI.

Later, Harbolt and I flew nearly every day following moonshiners and trip boys all over north Georgia. Most of this work involved major violator Charles Cargile. We had been trailing him for about two weeks when we finally followed one of his trip boys into a farm in Banks County around midnight.

"How about holding off checking that place till tomorrow night. I'd like to go with you," I asked Chuck Connor, who was working a conspiracy case on the Cargile group.

"Sure. Meet us at the usual place in Cornelia."

"Great! Thanks." It had been a while since I had helped raid a still and I didn't want to miss this one.

The next night, Connor, Harbolt, Elder, Rowden and I met the Gainesville agents on the ground next to the farm.

"The still's in that chicken house," whispered Agent Jim Strickland. "Bob Scott and the others are coming in at eleven o'clock."

I could hear the fuel oil burner roaring. At 10:30 P.M. a car pulled into the yard. I thought it was Scott and got ready for the chase. The car's lights went out. It turned around and backed up to the end of the chicken house. The driver beeped the horn twice and two big doors swung open. The 1956 Ford hot rod backed into the chicken house and the doors were closed.

"Just in time," I mused.

"Yeah, to get caught," added Elder.

At eleven o'clock, Scott wheeled into the yard and dropped an agent at the house. I made a break for the big doors on the end of the chicken house. Other agents came in from every direction. The moonshiners didn't have a chance. One managed to get to a back door, but that was all. We arrested Jewell Fingerhut, Bill Evans, Bo Robins, Felton Tillery and Gladys Price. It was a big outfit with more than 12,000 gallons of mash, a huge 3,200 gallon steel still and 2,000 gallons of moonshine ready to be hauled.

This was a lot more fun than studying rolls of film with a magnifying glass.

Carl Koppe, Richard Darby and John Rowden pour out moonshine while Ed Michaels and Jimmy Satterfield watch.

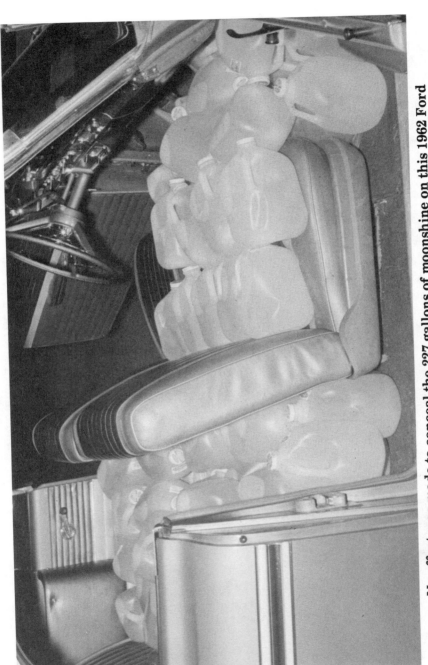

No effort was made to conceal the 227 gallons of moonshine on this 1962 Ford seized in Atlanta, Georgia.

ATF Agent Hugh Merrill at site of large illicit distillery, Lumpkin County, Georgia.

ATF Agent Jim Arey and State Agent Jones peer from under camouflage netting, Clayton County, Georgia.

27.

SLED ON HIS HEAD

JANUARY OF 1970 started off with a big ice storm in Atlanta, and flying weather was not so good. I was riding with my old partner Carl Koppe one night near Decatur when Jim Arey came on the ATF radio.

"Any unit near Glenwood Avenue—I've just jumped a carload on Candler Road. We just crossed Glenwood."

"This is 670. We're headed your way."

Koppe floorboarded the '68 Ford and we went screaming across town. Occasionally the ATF radio would come on momentarily and we could hear Arey's siren in the background.

"Where are you?" I asked.

No answer.

"You don't think he's wrecked, do you?" Koppe said.

"I sure hope not."

Just then we heard over the radio the whistling sound of heavy breathing—"Wheeze, wheeze. It's Willie (wheeze) Jarboe (wheeze, wheeze). He's on foot (wheeze). I lost him and had to (wheeze) come back to the car. He's (wheeze) wearing a dark brown jacket and has a toboggan on his head."

I looked at Koppe. "Did he say he had a sled on his head?"

"That's what it sounded like." Koppe was baffled. "Say again his description."

"(Wheeze) He's wearing a brown suede jacket and a toboggan on his head."

I gave Arey a weak 10-4. We found him standing by a liquor car loaded with 228 gallons of moonshine.

"It was Willie all right. I got close enough to recognize him but couldn't run him down," Arey explained excitedly.

"What was that you said he had on his head?" I asked.

"A toboggan—a winter knit cap. Don't you know what a toboggan is?" North Carolinian Arey was becoming irritated.

"I always thought it was a sled." Koppe and I burst into laughter as Arey stalked off.

People from different areas have a different jargon and way of describing things. The caps Arey was referring to are called "sock caps" in Georgia. They are known as watch caps in the Navy.

Another good example of this difference in language occurred the following month. Most of us were in Gainesville, Georgia attending U.S. District Court. To pass the time before our case was called we would sit in the courtroom and listen to other cases being tried.

Wally Hay, born and reared in New York City, was a typical New Yorker—quick witted, sharp, impatient and always in a hurry. He was just not accustomed to the way Southerners did things or to the way they said things. He had an especially hard time with the dialect of agents from Tennessee.

Bobby Cutshaw, an agent from east Tennessee, was on the witness stand that day. While being cross examined by a defense attorney Cutshaw was asked what the defendant in the case was wearing at the time of his arrest.

Bobby described the man's apparel. "Well, he was wearing blue jeans and a green flared shirt."

That night we were sitting in Cutshaw's room waiting while he took a shower. Hugh Merrill and Wally talked about Cutshaw's testimony.

"What did Bobby mean when he said that guy was wearing a flared shirt?" asked Wally.

"Aww—he meant he was wearing a *flowered* shirt. A shirt with flowers on it," replied Hugh, who had worked with Cutshaw for several years and understood his lingo.

"No, no—that's not what he said. He said it was flared. I heard him," argued Wally.

Hugh, knowing it was a waste of effort to argue with a New Yorker, simply called to Cutshaw in the bathroom. "Hey, Bobby—what comes out in the spring?"

After a few seconds, Cutshaw answered, "I don't know, FLARES, I guess."

So how smart you are just depends on what part of the country you're in.

✯ ✯ ✯

In the spring of 1970, Wally Hay was assigned to the new position of Airborne Operations Program

Leader so he could devote full time to the infrared experimental program and also start recruiting more special agent/pilots in the Southeast Region. I was getting more requests for aerial assistance than I could possibly handle, and our supervisors, Bill Griffin and Marvin Shaw were convinced of the need for pilots all over the southeast. We had proven that aerial surveillance was a successful technique and one against which the moonshiners had no defense. Once we got on them with the plane, they very seldom eluded us.

By the end of that year the infrared experiment was petering out. Bill Ivey, Dale Harbolt and Marshall Reece came on board as full-time special agent/pilots. Ivey remained in Tuscaloosa, Alabama to cover that section of the southeast. Harbolt was stationed in Atlanta to help me with some of the load there. Reece was transferred to Raleigh, North Carolina and soon became a legend in that area. His story, like that of so many other ATF agents, would fill a multi-volume work—and that would be hitting just the highlights.

After this realignment of personnel we began leasing four Cessna 172's on a yearly basis and everyone had plenty to do.

Give 'em the Business

Working as a full time special agent/pilot gave me the opportunity to work anywhere I was needed and to choose the jobs I thought would be the most productive. It was commonplace for me to work in every area of a state or in two or more states in one 24-hour period.

One morning in March I flew with Special Agent Arbie Odom in DeKalb, Henry, Spalding and Butts counties. We followed a 1962 Oldsmobile to a large distillery in the Ola section of Henry County. That afternoon I was flying with Bob Scott out of Gainesville and trailed a liquor car from a stash near Winder into Atlanta, where it was seized hauling 170 gallons of moonshine. Things were always hectic.

Even though I had been back in the regional office almost two years with flying as my prime responsibility, I continued working with the Atlanta agents. Jim Elder gave Dale Harbolt free rein to go with me as observer at any time.

Elder went with me when he could. The working relationships among the agents in Georgia and indeed most of the southeast couldn't have been better. Everyone was eager to use the airplane, and I was constantly on the go.

In April of 1970 Dale and I trailed Todd Brice, a liquor hauler from Dawsonville, to a huge distillery in a chicken house four miles northwest of Dahlonega. This one belonged to major violator Dick Truman. Two days later, Harbolt and I were circling slowly in the Dahlonega area at 10,000 feet. We had been working a big outfit in Paulding County and decided to check out the Lumpkin County area before we went in.

Suddenly the ATF radio blared. "670, are you in the area?"

Dale answered, "Ten-four, we're over the college."

"We've got movement up here at Dick's. Can you help us?" It was Bud Hazelip.

"We're on the way."

In two minutes we were over the chicken house.

"He's just leaving the yard," came Hazelip's whispered transmission. A white Ford Econoline was pulling onto the highway from the yard.

"We've got him," Harbolt said.

The truck headed south down 19.

"Looks like he's headed to Atlanta. You'd better see if you can get some Atlanta units to stand by," I suggested.

Harbolt got busy on the ATF radio. Carl Koppe, Ed Michaels and Chuck Stanfill were soon on the way. One car would be waiting at Roswell Road, the other at Sandy Springs.

By seven o'clock we reached the northwest section of Atlanta. Koppe and Stanfill were on the Econoline and we were running low on fuel.

"If you've got him, we'll pull off. You can knock him off any time now," I advised the ground units.

"Ten-four."

Ten minutes later Koppe came on the radio. "We stopped the truck and arrested Bruce Talley with 354 gallons. We appreciate the business."

28.
DIET DOCTOR

THERE WAS ALWAYS so much work to do, I would have embraced the idea of being twins if I could.

In the fall of 1970, Wally Hay was detailed to Washington, D.C. and later promoted to Special Agent in Charge in Philadelphia. Wally deserved the promotion.

I was assigned as Airborne Operations Leader and in February of 1971 the title became official, bringing with it the responsibility for ever-increasing paperwork.

After more than a year of testing, evaluation and limited success, we closed out the infrared program.

During this time several transcontinental airliners were hijacked and the public began clamoring for added security on planes, especially overseas flights. A joint security force was set up comprised of agents from ATF, Customs, IRS Intelligence, the Justice Department and a few from the military. The force was headed by ATF supervisor Arthur Monturi and was an immediate success. Most of these Sky Marshals were ATF agents. They were assigned to fly on transcontinental flights for a period of six months. There was little time for sightseeing because the schedule was a killer. Upon reaching London, they would be booked on a flight leaving within hours for Cairo. Once in Cairo, they would be on their way to Tokyo, and on and on.

My good friend Jimmy Satterfield was lucky enough to be assigned as a Sky Marshal and flew to every large city in the world. That was one detail I'm sorry I missed, but I was very much involved in flying at home. You can't have everything.

ATF had been given the responsibility of enforcing the Gun Control Act of 1968 and now with the assignment of additional enforcement duties relating to explosives and arson, the agency began to undergo growing pains. Its prime focus was starting to shift away from enforcing illegal liquor laws to the enforcement of gun and explosives laws.

The first week in December, ATF Agent Harry Lauderdale located a large trailer in the outskirts of Birmingham, Alabama loaded with explosive devices, chemicals and materials to make explosives and incendiary devices. There were hundreds of firearms parts and large amounts of extremist literature and instructions for making homemade bombs. Some of this material contained the name and address of a well-known diet doctor living in Birmingham.

On December 2, Special Agent John Rice called. "Charley, we need aerial photos of several farms in the Birmingham and Bessemer area. Can you help us out?"

"I'll be there as soon as the weather clears," I told him.

At ten that morning I took off in 7397 "Goober" from Fulton County Airport. I had to fly low to stay under the clouds as far as Anniston, but once I passed there, the clouds began to dissipate and I was soon in Birmingham. Rice met me at the airport.

"Charley, we've got a gun nut who is a well-known doctor in this area. He has numerous farms and we need to find the best access to them without being detected. I'm afraid this guy is connected with some violent people, so we need to be careful. We don't know how many weapons or explosive devices he may have. From the looks of the contents of the truck we seized it could be a lot." Rice was serious.

The next morning the sky had cleared and we spent several hours making aerial photos of three farms and the residence of the suspect. I left that afternoon with the film to be processed in the Atlanta Regional Office.

The next day Special Agent Ed Hughes, who later became Agent in Charge of the Organized Crime Branch in Washington, met me at the Fulton County Airport. The Explosives Control Act of 1970 had recently been enacted and this was to be one of the first cases made using these laws. Ed had assisted in the formulation and the wording of the act, furnishing information obtained from the U.S. Army EOD units. He had researched and provided information on various blasting agents, both commercial and homemade. John Rice called the regional office in Atlanta and suggested that Hughes assist in the investigation. Ed was assigned to help on the case due to his expertise and knowledge of the new law.

The trip to Birmingham was uneventful once Hughes, a giant of a man, wedged himself into the 172. He and Bill Griffin would have made a great pair of tight ends on any pro football team.

The next day we served a federal search warrant on the diet doctor's residence. In addition to a huge quantity of extremist literature, we found stacks and stacks of pornography. There were also huge barrels of diet pills in the basement, each containing some 50,000 amphetamine tablets, and all types of military artillery simulators (explosives) in addition to the truckload of arms.

The doctor was later convicted of the possession of explosives, blasting agents and chemicals to make explosives.

Moonshining was still a major problem in the southeast but one day in the not-too-distant future, it would be almost non-existent. ATF agents, myself included, would have some adjustments to make over the next ten years.

29.

MARENGO

REGIONAL SPECIAL AGENT Ed Gray had begun an extensive investigation of western North Carolina liquor law violators in February, 1970. Ed called me at home one morning in December.

"Charley, I've been working on Charles Lang for ten months. He is supposed to have a huge still set up somewhere near the Tennessee–Kentucky border. I know it sounds unusual for North Carolina violators to set up outside of their normal operating area, but this info comes from a man who should know."

"How can I help?" I asked.

"We're going to try to trail Lang with the plane. Jim Lancaster and Marshall Reece are working with me. If things get tight, I would like to have you on standby. It could turn out to be a long trail job. How about meeting me in Nashville tonight?"

"I'll be there."

In many cases the best-laid plans of officers do not pan out. Gray and I waited three days in Nashville. If Lang moved, we didn't know about it. It was almost Christmas, and Gray decided to break it off till after

New Year's Day. That suited me fine. At least I could spend a little time with my family.

The first week in January of '71 I was chomping at the bit to get back to work. The squad room phone rang.

"Squad room. Weems."

"Charley, this is Ed Gray. I'm in Louisville, Kentucky. Marshall Reece and I trailed Lang out of North Carolina and into an area near the Kentucky-Indiana line. Reece is beat. Can you bring a plane up here and help me?"

"Sure. I can leave in an hour and be there by three this afternoon."

"All right. Land at the main airport and give me a call on the ATF radio when you get close. I'll meet you and fill you in."

Gray had been trailing Lang and his girlfriend, trying to locate one of his illegal operations. Now with the help of an informer he was beginning to make a little progress. After days of waiting for something significant to happen, the break had finally come.

Gray didn't know of the origins of the distillery. Willie Clay and a partner had been running a big boiler distillery for over a year in the Wilkesboro area. They had made a lot of money from the operation. When Charles Lang approached them wanting to buy the outfit, they decided to sell. It was a good business decision that turned out to be bad luck for Clay. Someone broke into his house and stole much of the operating profit and all of the money from the sale of the distillery.

"They cleaned me out," Clay explained laconically some years later.

When I met Gray in Louisville I knew very little of what had happened previously. Gray brought me up to date on the progress of the case.

"Reece and I trailed Lang driving a big ten-wheel truck with ten tons of sugar from Goldsboro, N.C. to the Kentucky-Indiana border. The ground units saw Lang make a telephone call from a public booth at a big truck stop near the border. We had to pull off so the aircraft could be refueled and when we returned the truck had disappeared. So that's where we stand," Gray concluded.

"Let's go check that phone booth," I suggested. "Maybe we'll get lucky. Do we know the time the call was made?"

"Yeah. It was about 10:30 that night," replied Ed.

"Well, Ed, I don't know any telephone people in Indiana, but if the call was long distance, we may be able to find out who he called."

"Right. These badges we carry open a lot of doors. I just hope the telephone people will cooperate."

After retrieving the phone number from the booth, it was just a matter of finding the phone company office, getting in to see the proper person and hoping it would be someone sympathetic to law enforcement. In those days most people would help us if they possibly could.

In 15 minutes we learned the telephone number and with further discreet investigation found out the location of the phone Lang had called—a large farm in a remote area just out of Marengo, Indiana.

"I'm starving," Ed complained. "We haven't even eaten breakfast, and it's already lunchtime."

I was hungry, too. We stopped at a local diner. Gray ordered scrambled eggs, bacon and a bottle of Tabasco sauce. He covered his eggs with the red-hot sauce and commented, "Gives your food character." Ed had to have Tabasco with every meal.

As we drove through the beautiful rolling farmland of southern Indiana, I once again breathed a prayer, thanking the Lord for providing me with this job. Where else could a man find more fun and excitement?

We approached a small side road. "Is this the road?" Gray asked.

"I think so." I had been deep in thought. As we turned in to the narrow country road, the adrenalin started to flow once again.

"The man said we would cross a small wooden bridge over a railroad track and it would be the first driveway on the right," I said. "This looks like the place."

Ed eased the car across the wooden bridge and I peered down the tracks. Through the trees on the left side of the tracks I caught a glimpse of a big barn about 500 yards from us. I lost sight of the barn as we continued down the farm road.

"There's the drive on the right." Ed was getting excited now.

A farmhouse was barely visible some 300 yards off the public road.

"That's got to be it, Charley."

"Right."

We continued on past the driveway, discussing what to do next.

"You could drop me off at the railroad bridge and I could walk up the tracks and check it, but it would have to be after dark," I suggested.

Ed was thinking. "You know, we're out of our region and the higher-ups frown on our working in another region without prior approval. We'd better notify Bill Griffin in Regional Headquarters."

"Okay," I sighed, knowing he was right.

I headed back to Atlanta, disappointed.

Gray was anxious to start seeing results. Agents Art Bryant and Ed Garrison knew the North Carolina violators and were assigned to assist in the observation of the distillery. The Central Region furnished Area Supervisor Edgar Dillon and Agent Bill Tetterton. From the first week in January until January 17, agents Gray, Dillon, Bryant, Jesse Triplett and Paul Marshall made most of the ground observations.

The distillery was operated every night by Cal Marvin and Willard Raymond from about six o'clock until five the next morning. The still hands lived in the farmhouse and slept during the day, so most of the traffic to and from the barn was under cover of darkness. They would unload sugar, fuel oil and other materials at night and load the whiskey out at the same time.

When the distillery was raided on Sunday, January 17, 1971, officers arrested Cal Marvin and Willard Raymond in the barn operating the distillery. It was a huge outfit consisting of two 500-gallon steel stills,

67 wood barrel fermenters, three upright steam boilers and fuel oil burners and a large inventory of other distilling equipment and supplies. Two hundred forty gallons of moonshine were ready to be moved out.

In November of 1970, two months before we found the distillery, Kentucky Bureau of Transportation Inspectors Billy Martin and Joe Bacon stopped a heavily loaded truck driven by Willard Raymond. When Raymond refused to let the officers inspect his cargo, they became even more suspicious. They called Cave City, Kentucky Police Chief Ray Shaw, who contacted police in Rocky Mount, N.C. and inquired as to Raymond's record and reputation. They advised Shaw that Raymond was a convicted moonshiner who was probably hauling moonshine or materials to make it.

Chief Shaw obtained a search warrant for the truck and executed the warrant with Sheriff Cameron Poynter of Barnes County, Kentucky. They found 1,410 gallons of moonshine and arrested Raymond.

ATF Special Agent B.L. Bridgewater, working out of Bowling Green, Kentucky, was notified and he adopted the case for federal prosecution. He interviewed Raymond in Warren County Jail on November 22, five days after his arrest. Raymond called his wife in Rocky Mount while Bridgewater was there.

"Listen, you know who to get in touch with! You tell him that I'm getting damn tired of staying here in jail. If he don't get the money up here to get me out, the son of a bitch knows what's good for him. I'll give him 24 hours to get me out. You tell him that!"

After Raymond hung up he turned to Bridgewater. "The bastards—they just told my wife today I had been caught, and I've been in jail for five days."

Raymond was arrested again on January 14 near Frankfort, Ky. driving a truck carrying 1,164 gallons of moonshine from the Marengo still.

On February 14, 1971, several weeks after the distillery was seized, Bridgewater talked to Raymond again, this time in Rocky Mount, N.C.

"Listen, you don't know these people down here like I do. If I gave you a statement, they'll have me killed. The man wouldn't do it, but he would have it done.

"I'll tell you some of what I know but I'm not going to sign a statement."

"All right, I'm listening," Bridgewater encouraged him.

"Well, the still was moved into Indiana about a year ago. I didn't own the still, I was just working for the other man. I was being paid two dollars a case to haul the liquor. Occasionally I would help operate the still. We were making six gallons of moonshine every four minutes.

"I'll tell you one thing—if that had been my still I would be living a lot better than I am. I don't even own an automobile and Charles is driving a 1970 Continental."

After more discussion about his lawyer and getting his case moved to North Carolina for trial, Raymond ended the conversation by saying that if he decided to make a statement he would let the ATF agents know.

The first week in March, Bridgewater contacted Raymond again. "I've talked to another lawyer. The one they hired for me is just interested in protecting the people who are paying him. Don't let anyone know I've talked to you. They're all a little scared of me anyway," Raymond confided.

Three weeks later, on a dark night, a car pulled into Raymond's yard and the horn sounded. Raymond's wife was frightened.

"Don't worry. I'll just go see what they want," he assured her, and walked out to the car.

As she peeped past worn-out curtains, he called back to her, "I'll be back in a few minutes."

That was the last time she saw him alive.

Three days later Raymond's body was found in an abandoned well several miles from Rocky Mount. He had been shot in the back with a shotgun. A number of buckshot pellets had penetrated his back, ranging upward toward his head indicating he had been bending over when shot, either in a kneeling position or running with his head down.

Ed Gray worked hard with local officers to obtain sufficient evidence to indict the murderers, but no one was ever prosecuted and the case remains unsolved.

Raymond had nothing to do with ATF locating the distillery or the arrest of any of the moonshiners, but they thought he did. His murder served no purpose. In the end, major violator Charles Lang, his father Ron Lang and still hand Cal Marvin were all convicted of conspiring to produce, transport and sell illegal whiskey. They each received prison terms of three to five years.

This was yet another instance in which ATF agents encountered ruthless, cold-blooded criminals who would do anything to protect their monetary interest. They were neither small-time bootleggers nor innocent hill people struggling to put food on the table.

Although I had played only a small part in the investigation, it gave me a lot of satisfaction to know that the airplane and good common "horse sense" had helped us find another large illegal distillery. In the process our air operation began to get a little recognition outside the southeast.

"Four aces." ATF Agents King, Weems, Berry and Trickey.

30.
MIXED BLESSING

TIMES WERE CHANGING. Twenty years after being sworn in as a U.S. Treasury Agent, I was beginning to see a real change in ATF.

The outfit was finally getting some of the recognition it deserved but with that came the usual growing pains. In 1972 Alcohol, Tobacco and Firearms became a separate bureau under the Treasury Department. We no longer worked under the umbrella of the Internal Revenue Service and were now a distinct entity within the Department of the Treasury.

At the time most of us felt that this was what ATF had needed for years. In retrospect it appears to have been a mixed blessing. As ATF grew in stature as a separate bureau it became a target for people who would like to see it abolished.

We began devoting more and more time to firearms and explosives investigations. An average of one week per month was spent attending various schools learning how to identify and investigate bombings, arsons and militant groups.

The fun days of raiding stills and chasing liquor cars were coming to an end and are now a thing of the past for ATF agents. It was a sad day for me.

Most of the agents I talk about in *A Breed Apart* and *Agents That Fly* are now retired or fast approaching retirement. Several of them have recently died and most of their stories have gone with them to the grave. More than anything else, I hope that these few glimpses into their lives will help their families better understand the reasons for the long hours spent away from home and the dangers of the job they never revealed.

The fact that ATF was the "red-headed stepchild" of federal law enforcement has never deterred its agents from doing their jobs. Despite a great deal of criticism from the public, who never understood the magnitude of the problem moonshine caused, ATF agents have sacrificed their marriages, health and lives doing a job with very little praise, appreciation or recognition.

Knowing something of their dedication to their work may help the general public see that ATF agents have a legacy to be very proud of.

The ATF agent of today is better educated, better equipped and much better trained than the agents of my day.

Although the dangers inherent in enforcing any law in this country are far more widespread than when I was working, the agents of my time faced different types of dangers on a daily basis.

Recent events in Waco, Texas where ATF has been criticized and second-guessed by the news media, the National Rifle Association and others has made me proud of the caliber of present-day ATF agents.

They continue to be the highly motivated, show-no-quarter agent of the past, doing their jobs enforcing unpopular laws passed by Congress.

ATF agents are truly "A Breed Apart" but may, because of their dedication to enforcing these laws, become extinct.

If they do the country will lose one of the finest groups of people who ever wore a badge. I hope it never happens.

ATF Agents at 1963 pistol match at Atlanta Federal Penitentiary.

EPILOGUE

IN MY FIRST book, *A Breed Apart* and now in *Agents That Fly*, I have related true stories experienced by myself and other agents during the 1950's, 60's and 70's in the hope that the general public could get a better idea of the work ATF did.

The Bureau of Alcohol, Tobacco and Firearms has always been a unique federal law enforcement agency. It has had the responsibility of enforcing unpopular laws since its beginning but has performed the task with determination and dedication. Enforcing liquor laws is difficult, especially in the southeast where moonshiners have always been depicted as poor innocent mountain people struggling to feed their families. In most instances this was not true. When a distillery is producing 800 gallons of whiskey a day it is a big business.

When ATF began enforcing laws passed by Congress regulating the possession of machine guns and sawed-off shotguns, and especially after the assassination of President Kennedy and the enactment of the 1968 Gun Control Act, ATF was subject to constant criticism from various groups including the National Rifle Association.

Despite all the sniping and distorted stories promulgated by these groups, ATF agents have continued to do their jobs. Some have lost their lives in the process.

These are a few of the thousands of humorous, violent and gut-wrenching episodes that happened during the 1960's and 70's. If they give the reader some insight into the work done by the agents of that era along with some of the laughs, I have accomplished my goal.

Index